River of Dissolution:
D. H. Lawrence and
English Romanticism

River of Dissolution:

D. H. Lawrence & English Romanticism

COLIN CLARKE

NEW YORK

BARNES & NOBLE, INC.

Publishers & Booksellers since 1873

First published in Great Britain 1969
Published in the United States of America 1969
by Barnes & Noble, Inc., New York, N. Y.
© Colin Clarke 1969

Printed in Great Britain

'. . . *We always consider the silver river of life,*
rolling on and quickening all the world to a brightness,
on and on to heaven, flowing into a bright
eternal sea, a heaven of angels thronging.
But the other is our real reality—'

'*But what other? I don't see any other,*' *said Ursula.*

'*It is your reality, nevertheless,*' *he said;*
'*that dark river of dissolution . . .*'
                                    Women in Love

Contents

Introduction

The history of Lawrence criticism virtually begins with Middleton Murry's *Son of Woman*. In some ways Murry distorts grotesquely: where Lawrence imagines paradox his critic can see only duplicity. The book has been abused extravagantly, for all that, and needs to be recovered for Laurentian studies. Murry is aware, to the point of horror, that *Women in Love* discovers a virtue in degradation. What he shows no awareness of is Birkin's quest for wholeness—a wholeness to be achieved (or so it is implied at one level) by *incorporating* degradation. But at least Murry recognizes that Lawrence was attracted by the mud as well as repelled, so that for all the distortions, his book provides a better lead-in, at any rate to this novel if not to *The Rainbow*, than many a blander and seemingly saner study. What is really surprising is that the kind of critical enquiry Murry initiated should so rarely have been followed up; for after all Lawrence himself supplied indirect confirmation of its value—and something like a gloss on *Women in Love*—in those discursive writings of the period 1915–19 that find in corruption or disintegration an essential life-energy. So it has been one of my purposes in this book to show how the strange logic of *The Crown*, *The Reality of Peace* and the essay on Poe bears upon the major fiction.

There is an unintentional but neat exposure of the assumptions that lie behind a good deal of criticism of *Women in Love* in a review by Mark Spilka of *The Art of Perversity*, Kingsley Widmer's study of the *Tales*.[1] Spilka writes, dissentingly:

> There are Lawrence characters who destroy themselves by reaching nothingness and who assert 'perverse vitality' in their death throes. These disintegrating characters are cut off from the 'living cosmos', however,

and from vital human relations. They cannot be equated with integrating characters, those who seek rebirth through communion with man and nature. If the latter slough off conventional values, if they accept the necessity of emotional conflict and purgation, this does not make them perverse.

This lucid distinction between integrating and disintegrating characters, those who destroy themselves and those who don't, the vital and the perversely vital, is true to *Women in Love* at one level, and at another level as false as could well be. (It is also false to much in *The Rainbow*.) In his recent study of Lawrence, *Double Measure*, George Ford proposes to himself this question:

> . . . if the 'dreadful mysteries, far beyond the phallic cult' associated with the beetle-faced statue are represented in one scene as degenerate and in another scene (with only a slight shift in terminology) as redemptive—when Ursula is transfigured by her discovery of a 'source deeper than the phallic source'—how is a reader supposed to respond to what seems like a total contradiction?

The question is a good one (it had in fact been asked by Murry) but the answer, it must be said, can only mislead.

> What I have been stressing myself is that the complexities derive much of their density from Lawrence's choosing to portray Birkin in particular not as a White Knight, incorrupt and incorruptible, but as a suffering character dramatically involved in extricating himself from a death-loving world to which he is deeply, almost fatally, attracted. Like Conrad in similar presentation of Kurtz and Marlow, Lawrence in this way perhaps doubles the difficulties confronting his readers, but the clear gain in the overall effectiveness of his novel is beyond measurement. In a society made up of 'a herd of Gadarene swine, rushing possessed to extinction,' Gerald Crich is clearly infected with the madness and perishes. Birkin himself is a near casualty.

The opposition of corruption to non-corruption is assumed here to be final; Birkin must escape at all costs from a world in love with death. That the corruption might also be life-giving is not recognized as a relevant possibility. True, Professor Ford has a good deal to say about the way the novel obscurely endorses the degradation of Birkin himself.

But he nowhere suggests that this equivocal tolerance is in any sense extended to the decadence of the world that Birkin inhabits.

> We are being expected to discriminate between sensual experiences enjoyed by a pair of loving men and women (which are regarded by the novelist as innocently enjoyed) on the one hand, and degenerate indulgences of a society which has cut all connections with spiritual values on the other.

The discriminations the reader is required to make are surely more complex and demanding than this. The degenerate world which Birkin so reviles is beautiful as well as foul, and much of the novel is a haunting celebration of this beauty. The social decay, furthermore, is a potential source of life. On Professor Ford's reading however the society Lawrence presents is degenerate in the flattest and most absolute of senses, and grounds for hope are located entirely in the lovers ('. . . against a background of fetid corruption,' he remarks, 'a man and woman . . . discover each other, and their union establishes the possibility of hope and salvation').[2]

And this is representative. An article has appeared on *Pussum, Minette, and the Africo-Nordic Symbol in Lawrence's 'Women in Love'*,[3] and we might hope to find justice done there to the way the novel discourages simplistic attitudes towards the African process of disintegration. But the opening sentence already warns us that the profounder paradoxes will not come up for consideration:

> The crucial and controlling metaphor of D. H. Lawrence's
> *Women in Love* is a metaphor of destruction, that two-faced
> image of disintegration by heat and annihilation by cold.

Disintegration is a two-faced image in a far richer sense than this—a more intractable and disturbing sense too.

So *Women in Love* has suffered—whether the critical standpoint has been hostile or not. The common view among those who find the novel radically flawed is that the sanctioning of perversity and corruption is inadvertent; Lawrence sets Birkin up as the type of decency and sanity, but presents us instead with a hero who is demonstrably sick and depraved. Indeed the entire work, on this reading, is an expression of unacknowledged malaise and of a general tropism towards death. To answer this charge it is scarcely enough to show that the projection of Birkin's equivocal corruption is the work of an artist in evident control of his material. It needs to be demonstrated rather that paradoxes about corruption are dramatized at *every* level, that the strategy is directed *throughout* to affirming but also calling in question (often simultaneously) the dichotomies of decadence and growth, purity and degradation, the paradisal and demonic.

This reading, or something like it, has already commended itself in a number of quarters, though nowhere has it been fully elaborated. In *D. H. Lawrence: A Basic Study of his Ideas* (1955), Mary Freeman points out that 'need to absorb decay in an acceptable view of life became the dominant motivation in Lawrence's writing at this time' (that is, at the time of writing *Women in Love*): 'If the lotus has its roots in the mud, it has its flowers in the sun'. More recently Wilson Knight has declared,[4] finely, that in *Women in Love* Lawrence is trying 'to blast through . . . degradation to a new health'. And Mark Kinhead-Weekes, in much the same spirit, has noted how relevant to this novel is the 'new insight into "corruption" ' that we find articulated in the third essay of *The Crown:*

> The flux of corruption seems terrible to us, caught as we are in the perspective of time; but in itself it is not evil. It is necessary. . . . [What is being explored in this and the remaining essays is] the difference between a "flux of corruption" that is part of a divine process, and a vile and evil hardening into death that can know no rebirth.[5]

There is much in Kinhead-Weekes' interpretation to concur with, gratefully (above all, his recognition that the double attitude to corruption is no less central to *Women in Love* than it is to *The Crown* entails a perception that the African way is not unequivocally rejected), but there is also, I think, serious inaccuracy. I have in mind in particular his assumption that the process of reduction is conceived of by Lawrence as necessarily negative, a pure death-process; that Lawrence saw reductiveness, in fact, as the only evil.[6] Certainly *Women in Love* won't bear out this reading (the corruptive and reductive processes are assimilated to each other throughout, so if corruption is not inevitably or 'in itself' evil, nor is reduction), and *The Crown* won't either:

> Leonardo knew this: he knew the strange endlessness of the flux of corruption . . . the phosphorescence of corruption, the salt, cold burning of the sea which corrodes all it touches, coldly reduces every sun-built form to ash, to the original elements. This is the beauty of the swan, the lotus, the snake, this cold white salty fire of infinite reduction. And there was some suggestion of this in the Christ of the early Christians, the Christ who was the Fish.
> . . . All birth comes with the reduction of old tissue. But

the reduction is not the birth. That is the fallacy of all of us, who represent the old tissue now.

There are complexities here in face of which the commentary Kindhead-Weekes has to offer provides little help.

More persuasive is Frank Kermode's recent essay, *Lawrence and the Apocalyptic Types*,[7] where there is full recognition of the difficulty of distinguishing in *Women in Love* between the reductiveness that makes for death and the reductiveness that makes for life.

> The real descent into hell and rebirth Lawrence can signify only by sex. The purest expression of it is in *The Man Who Died*, but in some ways the love-death undergone by Ursula and Connie is a fuller image because it amalgamates heaven and hell, life-flow and death-flow, in one act. The act is anal . . . This participation in 'dreadful mysteries beyond the phallic cult', enacts death and rebirth at once, is decadent and renovatory at once.
>
> As the literature shows, this is not easy to discuss. One cannot even distinguish, discursively, between the sex Gudrun desires from Loerke, which is obscene and decadent, and that which Ursula experiences with Birkin, which is on balance renovatory. The first comes straight out of Nordau, the second is darkly millennialist, again like that of some medieval sects in their Latter Days; yet in practice they presumably amount to almost the same thing. It is an ambivalence which may have characterized earlier apocalyptic postures, as Fraenger argues in his book on Hieronymus Bosch. Decadence and renovation, death and rebirth, in the last days, are hard to tell apart, being caught up in the terrors.

Not only is the renovatory virtue of the decadence emphasised, but, negatively and equally important, no distinction is drawn, by implication, between the corruptive process and the process of reduction.

So the moralistic interpretation of Lawrence's fiction that has prevailed for at least two decades shows signs of cracking.* Nevertheless,

* Kingsley Widmer's study, *The Art of Perversity*, should also be mentioned here, though it is not concerned with Lawrence's novels. Arguing that our traditions of intellectual and emotional perversity have been an inadequately acknowledged and insufficiently valued part of our sensibility, Widmer has explored the demonic and nihilistic implications of the shorter fictions. The general intention of the book is admirable, even if the particular valuations are not often easy to accept. (Mark Spilka justly observes in the review already cited that 'Widmer plays too glibly with the ambiguities of perversity', 'favours shock-vocabulary' and 'anti-social toughness', and is guilty, altogether, of 'reverse sentimentality'.)

considerable demolition work remains to be done. The decisive critical influence throughout this period has of course been that of Leavis, whose insistence on Lawrence's moral centrality has proved as misleading as illuminating. There is much even in *The Rainbow* to which the interpretation he has popularized, focussed as it is on 'the pieties and continuities of life', on communal traditions and their fictive embodiment, has no relevance. It is his reading of *Women in Love* however that fails most often to satisfy.

> The West African statuette (this we are actually told, and the local explicitness merely picks up what has been done in drama, imagery and poetic organization) represents something that we are to see as a default, a failure, antithetical—and so significantly related—to the human disaster enacted by Gerald Critch. A strong normative preoccupation, entailing positives that are correctly present in many ways (we have them above in the phrases, 'the goodness, the holiness, the desire for creation and productive happiness') informs the life of *Women in Love*— the life that manifests itself in the definition and 'placing' of these opposite human disasters.

How much this leaves out of account, I hope to show. The satanic Lawrence, or the Lawrence who finds beauty in the phosphorescence of decay, will be sought in vain in the pages of *D. H. Lawrence: Novelist*.

Here then is a situation which would seem to leave room for numerous critical studies, let alone one. But there is a further gap to be filled: virtually nothing has been written on Lawrence's debt as a novelist to the English Romantic poets.[8] It is a theme that has close affinities with the one I have been considering—the ambivalence of Lawrence's attitude to corruption. In a late essay he wrote:

> For the truth is, we are perishing for lack of fulfilment of our greater needs, we are cut off from the great sources of our inward nourishment and renewal, sources which flow eternally in the universe. Vitally, the human race is dying. It is like a great uprooted tree, with its roots in the air. We must plant ourselves again in the universe.

The notion of being planted in the universe is thoroughly Romantic of course and Birkin's conception of 'the fall' in the chapter 'Moony' would seem to belong very directly to this organicist tradition:

> There is a long way we can travel, after the death-break: after that point when the soul in intense suffering breaks,

breaks away from its organic hold like a leaf that falls. We
fall from the connexion with life and hope, we lapse from
pure integral being, from creation and liberty, and we fall
into the long, long African process of purely sensual
understanding, knowledge in the mystery of dissolution.

The antithesis is a sharp one: the creative and living over against death,
corruption, disconnexion. The assumptions would seem to be all of the
organicist or Wordsworthian kind; we die if we fail to sustain the living
connexion with a universe that is holy. But Birkin is not consistent—as
I have already implied; the tenor of his reflections elsewhere would lead
us to infer that to belong means to establish communion with life-
energies or sources of power that are, equally, corrupted and incorruptible.* Tension of this kind should not however surprise the reader
of English Romantic poetry. If Nature is uncorrupted in the poetry of
Wordsworth it both is and is not in the poetry of Coleridge, or Shelley;
it is not through acknowledging only the beauty and holiness of God's
universe that the Ancient Mariner achieves his precarious redemption.
And so in *Women in Love*. Throughout the novel there is a running
debate between two conceptions of atonement; we lapse from true
singleness—remain fixed in deadly isolation—if we cut ourselves off
from energies conceived of as corruptive and paradisaically pure.

* Compare 'the fountain of mystic corruption' (p. 343) and 'the
fountain-head was incorruptible' (p. 538). Page numerals throughout this
book refer to the 1960 Penguin edition.

Part One
'Dissolve, and quite forget':
A Tradition of Metaphor

'Fade far away, dissolve, and quite forget
What thou among the leaves hast never known.'
                              Ode to a Nightingale

'There is in me the desire of creation and the desire
of dissolution. Shall I deny either ? Then neither
is fulfilled.'
                              The Reality of Peace

I Self-destroying

It is poetry that gives 'the ultimate shape to one's life', after all; poetry 'woven deep' into consciousness in the early years. So Lawrence testified towards the close of his career,[1] though it was in the course of making the 'almost shameful' admission that the poems which had meant most to him were 'still not woven so deep . . . as the rather banal nonconformist hymns that penetrated through and through' his childhood.

Among the few poems he mentions as having been specially meaningful are 'Wordsworth's *Ode to Immortality*' [*sic*] and the Odes of Keats. One would have known however, without this testimony, that the English Romantics had made a deep impression on him; for the extraordinary abundance in his own writing of images of dissolution—swooning, fading, lapsing out, dissolving, decomposing—in itself provides sufficient proof that he had their poetry in his bones. Like the Romantics Lawrence is endlessly concerned with what Keats had called 'self-destroying'*— the process of dying into being, the lapsing of consciousness which is yet the discovery of a deeper consciousness, the dissolution of the hard, intact, ready-defined ego:

> You've got to lapse out before you can know
> what sensual reality is, lapse into unknowingness,

* The expression occurs in *Edymion*, Book I (I discuss the passage later). Wordsworth uses the word too at the end of the Book VII of *The Prelude*, and in a context concerned with a process of diffusion, or interfusion—that is, a process analogous to that of dissolution:

> The Spirit of Nature was upon me here;
> The Soul of Beauty and enduring life
> Was present as a habit, and diffused,
> Through meagre lines and colours, and the press
> Of self-destroying, transitory things
> Composure and ennobling Harmony. (1805: VII, 735–40)

3

and give up your volition. You've got to do it.
You've got to learn not-to-be, before you can
come into being.

So Birkin assures Ursula; and we are clearly invited to concur. But *Women in Love* is concerned with more than one kind of self-destruction. The novel makes no pat contribution to single-mindedness, and the activity of dissolution is conceived of throughout as reductive and lethal as well as liberating and redemptive. We recall the dissolution that Hermione experiences in her duel with Birkin at Breadalby, or the subterranean desire felt by Gerald and Gudrun 'to fling away everything and *lapse* into a sheer unrestraint, brutal and licentious'; or that equivocal process that brings to Gerald, lying in Gudrun's arms, an influx of power at once illusory and real: 'He felt himself dissolving and sinking to rest in the bath of her living strength'.

In the poetry of the Romantics analogous complexities and dubieties are to be found on all sides. Dissolution as the melting away of the body in visionary rapture, dissolution as the deprivation of consciousness in sleep or trance, dissolution as decomposition, dissolution as death: these motifs are woven together in Romantic poetry habitually (*Ode to a Nightingale* is perhaps the *locus classicus*), even though the word 'dissolve' (or a cognate term) is not necessarily itself invoked. In *The Reality of Peace* Lawrence declares:

> If there is no autumn and winter of corruption, there is
> no spring and summer. All the time I must be dissolved
> from my old being.[2]

That shift from 'corruption' to 'dissolved', so characteristic of Lawrence, has behind it a corpus of poetry whose ambiguous rhythms associate in a thousand devious ways the potentialities of life *and* death in the manifold activities of dissolution. So the Mariner's acceptance of the natural world entails an acceptance not only of the water-snakes but of all the corruption of the rotting deep; and this acceptance is at the same time a dissolving, or partial dissolving, of his old being—signalled, at the climacteric moment, by a lapsing away of consciousness.

II Images of dissolution in
Burke's Enquiry

A cursory reference to the O.E.D. will confirm how the meanings of 'dissolution' (and its analogues) could become polarized, suggesting possibilities of corruption and idealism alike.

> *Dissolve* (trans.) to disintegrate, decompose; to melt or reduce into a liquid condition; to relax or enervate with pleasure; to release, set free; to release from life, cause the dissolution or death of; to destroy; (intrans.) to lose its integrity, to become liquid.

To lose integrity—to be set free: the two conceptions indicate the poles between which the energy of Lawrence's art is generated again and again. And yet, in acknowledging the polarity we acknowledge too a unity: the liberating and the reducing are both activities of dissolution, modes of a process to which Lawrence can still, convincingly, give a single name.

The reason he can do so becomes clear, I think, if we trace the history of the word dissolve (and its analogues) back through the Romantics to the Eighteenth Century. For the extraordinary proliferation of images of dissolution in the Romantic period, the manifold uses to which they are put and also the tendency for their meanings or values to polarize, has a good deal to do with the fact that English Romanticism was nourished in important respects by eighteenth-century empiricism and sensationism. Notoriously, the notion that the mind, in acquiring the materials for reflection, is completely passive was an axiom of eighteenth-century thinking; perceiving entails, in the first place, submission to an influx of sensation. How a climate of opinion in which this notion is a *donnée* could make available for Romantic poetry the affiliated images in which I am interested is demonstrated by a sequence of argument in Burke's *Enquiry*. Part IV Section XIX bears the caption 'the physical cause of love' and runs as follows:

> When we have before us such objects as excite love and complacency, the body is affected, so far as I could observe, much in the following manner. The head reclines something on one side; the eyelids are more closed than usual, and the eyes roll gently with an inclination to the object, the mouth is a little opened, and the breath drawn slowly, with now and then a low sigh: the whole body is composed, and the hands fall idly to the sides. All this is accompanied with an inward sense of melting and languor. These appearances are always proportioned to the degree of beauty in the object, and of sensibility in the observer. And this gradation from the highest pitch of beauty and sensibility, even to the lowest of mediocrity and indifference, and their correspondent effects, ought to be kept in view, else this description will seem exaggerated, which it certainly is not. But from this description it is almost impossible not to conclude, that beauty acts by relaxing the solids of the whole system. There are all the appearances of such a relaxation; and a relaxation somewhat below the natural tone seems to me to be the cause of all positive pleasure. Who is a stranger to that manner of expression so common in all times and in all countries, of being softened, relaxed, enervated, dissolved, melted away by pleasure?

This foreshadows the way in which images of dissolution were to ramify in the Romantic period. It is not that there is anything novel or distinctively Romantic (or pre-Romantic) in the mere association of pleasure, particularly the pleasure of love, with dissolution and the sense of relaxation; on the contrary, as Burke points out, the association is an ancient one, and certainly instances of it may be found in English poetry before the middle of the eighteenth century, notably in the work of Crashaw. But no writer before had made such play with these concepts as Burke does here or had discovered such a range of experiences or topics to which they might seem relevant. The *Enquiry*, as the full title proclaims, is philosophical in one of the old-fashioned senses of that word: Burke is trying to explain a wide diversity of phenomena in terms of as few principles as possible. *All* pleasure soothes, mollifies, relaxes—

this general principle he both arrives at empirically and applies *a priori*; and by means of it he finds a common physiological denominator in pleasures as apparently remote as eating sweets and contemplating a beautiful landscape. In effect he is anatomising the internal relationships of a single corpus of affiliated imagery. We are witnessing the emergence of a metaphor that was to prove no less significant in the Romantic era than that other radical metaphor of the growing plant.

In Section XXI, entitled 'Sweetness, its nature', Burke has something to say about the connection between, on the one hand, relaxation and the 'weak cohesion of the component parts of any body' (or in other words 'a body's tendency to dissolve') and on the other hand 'fluidity'—a connection which, as the title of this book suggests, is vital in the tradition of Romantic imagery with which I am concerned.

> For as fluidity depends, according to the most general opinion, on the roundness, smoothness, and weak cohesion of the component parts of any body; and as water acts merely as a simple fluid; it follows, that the cause of its fluidity is likewise the cause of its relaxing quality; namely, the smoothness and slippery texture of its parts.

Burke does little more than this to associate fluidity and dissolution, but the passage is a portent. (There is a work of the same period as the *Enquiry* in which the associating of dissolution and pleasure with fluidity is recurrent and obvious. I refer to Cleland's *Memoirs of a Woman of Pleasure.* The following is sufficiently typical:

> But, when successive engagements had broke and inur'd me, I began to enter into the true unallay'd relish of that pleasure of pleasures, when the warm gush darts through all the ravish'd inwards; what floods of bliss! what melting transports! what agonies of delight! too fierce, too mighty for nature to sustain; well has she therefore, no doubt, provided the relief of a delicious momentary dissolution, the approaches of which are intimated by a dear delirium, a sweet thrill on the point of emitting those liquid sweets, in which enjoyment itself is drown'd, when one gives the languishing stretch-out, and dies at the discharge.

For all the differences, this has obvious points of contact with *Women in Love*, where the imagery of dissolution often implies unobtrusively the notion of a seminal flow.)

7

Throughout Sections XIX, XX and XXI and in the *Enquiry* as a whole, Burke's theorising is characteristic of an age whose philosophers took for granted the passivity of the mind in sensation.* Just as, for Locke and later phenomenalists, 'ideas' are 'let into' the mind or 'received' by it via the senses, so for Burke pleasure is conceived of in terms of yielding, passiveness, relaxation. It is an attitude that persists into the Romantic period. For all their emphasis on the activity and creativeness of the mind the Romantics paid due tribute to the value of passivity, not only in the perception of beauty but in the perception of truth. Indeed this is pre-eminently the period in which it is recognized that there are kinds of truth inaccessible to an alert and strenuous consciousness.

Not that the Romantics took Burke's aesthetic to their hearts. Wordsworth and Coleridge both, in fact, had a low opinion of the *Enquiry*;[3] yet the intellectual climate in which they grew up was after all Burke's too, and without invoking any crude mechanics of transmission we can affirm that in certain important ways they share his vocabulary. For a psychology or a literature that is deeply concerned with the response of the five senses to the natural world, and which attaches full or even excessive importance to the passive and receptive functions of the human mind, will always be likely to draw, for its varied rhetorical purposes, on images of dissolution. It is not simply chance that Burke, Wordsworth, Coleridge, Shelley, Keats and Lawrence should all rely on these images in varying degrees: it is a direct consequence of the importance they attach to the notion of *yielding* to the influx of sensation, passion, beauty and (Burke is an exception here) truth.

But there were of course important elements in the Romantic climate of thought which are not to be found even in embryo in Burke's writings. As an aesthetician and psychologist he is resolutely literal-minded, a sensationist of a most uncompromising kind: 'When we go but one step beyond the immediately sensible qualities of things, we go out of our depth', he declares. It was a Romantic rather than an

---

* Compare Addison (*Spectator* 411): 'It is but opening the eye, and the scene enters'. In a later essay (*Spectator* 580) we learn that the senses are 'inlets of great pleasure to the soul'. The passivity of the imaginative process in Addison's aesthetic is well brought out by Ernest Tuveson in *The Imagination as a Means of Grace* (C.U.P. 1960). However, it is also Tuveson's object to show how Addison's aesthetic tends to be modified in certain quarters as the century progresses, and a more active role given to the imagination.

eighteenth-century habit of mind that forged linguistic ties not only between aesthetic contemplation, sleep, eroticism and dissolution, but between all these and death, or corruption. (In *Clarissa Harlowe* we find already a Romantic *patterning*: love, passivity, death. What we do not find is a Romantic vocabulary—the characteristic language of dissolution.)

III *Abstraction and decay*

One of the equations most commonly established in Romantic poetry (the idiom of Empson insists on its appropriateness) is that between dissolution as sublimation and dissolution as corruption.

> O Wild West Wind, thou breath of Autumn's being,
> Thou, from whose unseen presence the leaves dead
> Are driven, like ghosts from an enchanter fleeing,
>
> Yellow, and black, and pale, and hectic red,
> Pestilence-stricken multitudes: O thou,
> Who chariotest to their dark wintry bed
>
> The winged seeds, where they lie cold and low,
> Each like a corpse within its grave, . . .

The image of vegetable corruption no less than the image of growth witnesses to the dominance in the period of organicist habits of thought. Here we have something different from the charnel-house imagery—unmodulated Gothic—that crops up fairly frequently in the earlier Shelley; and the something different is distinctively Romantic. But equally distinctive is the way images of corruption and vegetable decay modulate into images suggestive of tenuity and spirituality. The dead leaves suddenly become ghosts, a deprivation of substance which does not prevent their also being pestilence-stricken multitudes. With the wisdom of hindsight we see how this conjunction of the decaying and the disembodied anticipates important resonances in *Women in Love*, and we realize that Birkin's vision of 'knowledge in dissolution and corruption' has a richer historical relevance than it appears at first sight to lay claim to.

For it is one of the distinctions of *Women in Love* that it correlates, convincingly, on the one hand the fascination with corruption and on the other the impulse towards the ideal (in the sense of the abstract or unbodied).* In its immediate context the phrase 'knowledge in dissolution and corruption' would seem to apply merely to 'the long African process', 'mindless progressive knowledge through the senses'. But it is also deeply if more obliquely relevant to that alternative process of degeneration that Birkin goes on at once to consider: the Nordic way, the 'mystery of ice-destructive knowledge, snow-abstract annihilation'.

> This was why her face looked like a beetle's: this was why the Egyptians worshipped the ball-rolling scarab: because of the principle of knowledge in dissolution and corruption. . . . There remained this way, this awful African process, to be fulfilled. It would be done differently by the white races. The white races, having the Arctic north behind them, the vast abstraction of ice and snow, would fulfil a mystery of ice-destructive knowledge, snow-abstract annihilation. Whereas the West Africans, controlled by the burning death-abstraction of the Sahara, had been fulfilled in sun-destruction, the putrescent mystery of sun-rays.

A conveniently brief gloss on 'snow-abstract annihilation' is provided by a passage in *The Rainbow*:

> How terrible it was! There *was* a horrible fascination in it—human bodies and lives subjected in slavery to that

* The correlation is not to be found in *Women in Love* only of course, though there it is established with a notable comprehensiveness. Here is an analogous and characteristic passage from a non-fictional context:

> And now, man has begun to be overwhelmingly conscious of the repulsiveness of his neighbour, particularly of the physical repulsiveness. There it is, in James Joyce, in Aldous Huxley, in André Gide, in modern Italian novels like *Parigi* —in all the very modern novels, the dominant note is the repulsiveness, intimate physical repulsiveness of human flesh. It is the expression of absolutely genuine experience. What the young feel intensely, and no longer so secretly, is the extreme repulsiveness of other people.
> It is, perhaps, the inevitable result of the transcendental bodiless brotherliness and social 'adhesiveness' of the last hundred years. People rose superior to their bodies, and soared along, till they had exhausted their energy in this performance. The energy once exhausted, they fell with a struggling plunge, not down into their bodies again, but into the cesspools of the body.[4]

II

> symmetric monster of the colliery. There was a swooning, perverse satisfaction in it. For a moment she was dizzy. Then she recovered . . .
>
> But her Uncle Tom and her mistress remained there among the horde, cynically reviling the monstrous state and yet adhering to it, like a man who reviles his mistress, yet who is in love with her. . . . His real mistress was the machine, and the real mistress of Winifred was the machine. She too, Winifred, worshipped the impure abstraction, the mechanisms of matter. There, there, in the machine, in service of the machine, was she free from the clog and degradation of human feeling. There, in the monstrous mechanism that held all matter, living or dead, in its service, did she achieve her consummation and her perfect unison, her immortality.

We observe here the secret affinities between the Nordic and the African ways; for 'the swooning, perverse satisfaction', the subjection in slavery (we recall that, later, Minette is subjected and slavish) hint at mindless and regressive sensuality, while the worship of the pure abstractions of matter and machine speaks of the snow-abstract North. In *Women in Love* this implicating of sensual perversity and the flight into abstraction is far more thorough. Gerald and Gudrun worship the flesh in death (the episode in 'Rabbit' alone gives proof of it); but also, fascinated by the mechanisms of matter, they seek to *free* themselves from the flesh, Gerald from the clog of the flesh and Gudrun from its degradation.

It has been observed (and after all it is obvious enough) that *Women in Love* focusses with a decisive placing effect the death-loving tendencies in West European culture—which is to say, nineteenth-century Romantic culture. (Gerald and Gudrun, we are told explicitly by Birkin, are *fleurs du mal*). And yet in the last analysis the bearing the novel has upon the European Romantic tradition is less significant than the bearing it has on *English* Romanticism—by which, as I have indicated, I mean English Romantic poetry. In *Introduction to These Paintings* Lawrence is found declaring:

> Water-colour will always be more of a statement than an experience.
>
> And landscape, on the whole, is the same. It doesn't call up the more powerful responses of the human imagination, the sensual, passional responses. Hence it is the favourite modern form of expression in painting. There is no deep conflict. The instinctive and intuitional

consciousness is called into play, but lightly, superficially.
It is not confronted with any living, procreative body.
Hence the English have delighted in landscape, and have
succeeded in it well. It is a form of escape for them from
the actual human body they so hate and fear, and it is an
outlet for their perishing aesthetic desires.

. . . And, especially, art must provide that escape. It is
easy in literature. Shelley is pure escape: the body is
sublimated into sublime gas. Keats is more difficult—the
body can still be *felt* dissolving in waves of successive
death—but the death-business is very satisfactory.[5]

It is the usual pattern: dissolution as disembodiment and dissolution as
the reduction of the flesh, and both seen as essentially English-Romantic.
Yet it is not of course to English Romanticism only that Lawrence applies
these categories; it is in just these terms of a dual movement towards
sublimation *and* corruption, abstraction *and* decay that, repeatedly, he
diagnoses the malaise of European culture in general. But one has every
right to infer that the broader diagnostic understanding was the fruit of
a long inwardness with Romantic culture at home and, more specifically,
with native Romantic poetry.

And yet there is a sense in which the extent of Lawrence's indebtedness to the English Romantics is a matter for conjecture. There must of
course be something conjectural about determining the extent of *any*
literary influence. It is not this general and inevitable uncertainty I have
in mind however, but the special difficulty of disentangling Lawrence's
debt to English Romanticism from his debt to Christianity. For the
language in which he formulates his objection to the one is virtually
interchangeable with the language in which he judges the other (the
compulsion to judge being itself a token of sustained influence.) It is a
crippling deficiency in Graham Hough's discussion of Lawrence's
'Quarrel With Christianity', in his study *The Dark Sun*, that it should be
concerned exclusively with Lawrence's notion that Christianity is an
attempt 'to live from the love-motive alone', and that Christian *caritas* is
disembodied, 'cut off from the natural carnal roots of love', and as a
consequence 'kept going by a barren effort of will'. For this is to fail to
respond to the inner dialectic whereby Christianity in its idealistic or
disembodied mode is seen to entail precisely its opposite, a worship of
the flesh-in-reduction, a diseased and hectic functioning of the senses.
The validity of Lawrence's 'ideas' about Christianity is not here an issue;
I am simply concerned to establish the resemblance between his critique
of Christianity and his critique of Romanticism, and to show the bearing

they both have upon the radical polarity of abstraction and decay. Illustrations from the major novels, *Women in Love* in particular, spring easily to mind. The dissociated condition of Halliday, for instance, is only an extreme instance of a general malaise:

> 'Of course,' he said, 'Julius is somewhat insane. On the one hand he's had religious mania, and on the other, he is fascinated by obscenity. Either he is a pure servant, washing the feet of Christ, or else he is making obscene drawings of Jesus—action and reaction—and between the two, nothing. He is really insane. He wants a pure lily, another girl, with a Botticelli face, on the one hand, and on the other, he *must* have Minette, just to defile himself with her.'

Will Brangwen, in *The Rainbow*, seems remote enough from Halliday, certainly; yet there is a sense in which they can be said at least to breathe the same air. On the one hand he can lose himself in a mystical sexual consummation (in Lincoln Cathedral) and on the other (this at any rate is how Anna sees it, when they argue about the Pietà) he worships the body in death: sublimation and death-worship entail each other.

> 'You see, it means the Sacraments, the Bread,' he said, slowly.
> 'Does it!' she cried. 'Then it's worse. *I* don't want to see your chest slit, nor to eat your dead body, even if you offer it to me. Can't you see it's horrible?'

So too, returning to *Women in Love*, Mr Crich's pure Christian altruism involves as a natural corollary the lethal perversity of his son.

And this is the dialectic of Romanticism also. For Lawrence, *the* Christian-Romantic (the formula is justified though Lawrence himself never used it) was Dostoievsky, and in commenting on the contemporary Dostoievsky-cult and on the novels themselves he comes back again and again to the unhealthy combination of dirt and purity, ecstasy and corruption, death-worship and the mania to be God, absolved from all relation.

> I don't like Dostoievsky. He is again like the rat, slithering along in water in the shadows, and, in order to belong to the light, professing love, all love. But his nose is sharp with hate, his running shadowy and rat-like, he is a will fixed and gripped like a trap, He is not nice![6]
> Petronius is straight and above board. Whatever he does, he doesn't try to degrade and dirty the pure mind in him. But Dostoievsky, mixing God and sadism, he is foul.[7]

On the other hand, in *Women in Love* itself the attempt to synthesize purity and degradation is crucial; clearly Lawrence is fascinated by what he attacks. (Not, of course, that he was quite unaware of, or never acknowledged, the fascination.)* And we note that *The Idiot* is the novel of Dostoievsky's he likes best, because to him it seems to bear out so emphatically the case against Christianity:

> I like *The Idiot* best. The Idiot is showing the last stage of Christianity, of becoming purely self-less, of becoming disseminated out into a pure, absolved consciousness. This is the Christian ecstasy, when I become so transcendently super-conscious that I am bodiless, that the universe is my consciousness. This is the little Idiot prince. It is the ecstasy of being devoured in the body, like the Christian lamb, and of transcendence in the consciousness, the spirit.[8]

For 'the little Idiot prince' one might read Shelley,† or (if less obviously) any other of the great English Romantics.

* In a letter to Catherine Carswell, 2 Dec. 1916, he writes:

> . . . don't think I would belittle the Russians. They have meant an enormous amount to me; Turgenev, Tolstoi, Dostoievski—mattered more than almost anything, and I thought them the greatest writers of all time.

And the scattered references to Dostoievsky in *Phoenix*, though abusive for the most part, have, again, the compensatory note of admiration: he is a 'great nervous genius', 'an evil thinker and a marvellous seer', and so on.

† The poem of Shelley's that perhaps bears most directly upon topics raised in this and succeeding sections is *The Sensitive Plant*. The sharp conjunction of disembodiment and decay; the emphatic transcendentalism on the one hand and the strange, inverse endorsement of natural process and corruption on the other; idealism yielding to a sick and lurid physicality, so that, for all the concluding 'doctrine', the one seems to be secretly *responsible* for the other, as well as overtly opposed to it: this may all be said, legitimately, to be representative 'source material' for *Women in Love*. (To what extent Shelley's handling of the theme is ironic is a nice question. See below pp. 41–2.)

IV Living disintegration

It is considerations of this kind indeed that lead one inevitably to the judgment that, by comparison with his debt to the poets, Lawrence's debt to the organicist social philosophers—Coleridge, Carlyle, Ruskin—is a minor affair. This indebtedness has its significance for the student of his art, certainly; but the significance can easily be exaggerated.[9] For in the writings of the 'philosophers' there is none of that cross-fertilizing of the vocabulary of corruption and the vocabulary of dissolution so characteristic of the poets and Lawrence alike. In exposing the malaise of a disintegrated culture—communal life subjected more and more to the principles of mathematics and mechanics—the philosophers used the language of organicism in a rhetoric of sheer rejection; and though Lawrence does so too from time to time, as in the following passage from *Women in Love*, he is apt to sound one-noted where this rhetoric is not countered by forces that make for dubiety and tension.

> It was the first great step in undoing, the first great phase of chaos, the substitution of the mechanical principle for the organic, the destruction of the organic purpose, the organic unity, and the subordination of every organic unit to the great mechanical purpose. It was pure organic disintegration and pure mechanical organization. This is the first and finest state of chaos.

This steep contrast of life and the machine, or the organic and the disintegrated, is true to the spirit of the novel at one level only, and that not the most important. What is more characteristic is the art that leaves us in doubt whether the inverse process of disintegration or corruption is not as life-enhancing as the positive, organic process. And if Lawrence found any encouragement in earlier literature to advance this paradox in terms of the radical metaphor of dissolution, it is in English Romantic

16

poetry that he would have found it. (This claim needs to be buttressed with more argument and illustration than I have yet provided, but I waive this consideration for the moment.)

Whether the debt to the poets is acknowledged or not, the ambivalence of Lawrence's attitude to corruption is indisputable. The Dictionary, we have seen, gives decomposition as one of the head-meanings of dissolution, and it is as though, in some of the essays and in *Women in Love*, Lawrence set out to articulate deliberately all the implications of that equation. True, the Lawrence who most counts in the popular imagination is the Lawrence who made an uncompromising distinction between organic sex or blood-passion on the one hand and mechanical or disintegrative sex on the other.

> Personal or nervous or spiritual sex is destructive to the blood, has a katabolistic activity, whereas coition in warm blood-desire is an activity of metabolism. . . . The disintegrative effect of modern sex-activity is undeniable. It is only less fatal than the disintegrative effect of masturbation, which is more deadly still.[10]

It is the tension however between this Lawrence and the other, more paradoxical Lawrence (who has received far less attention) that does so much to account for the achievement in the novels and tales. And also for the achievement in more discursive modes. Where Lawrence is engaged with paradoxes about reduction there is always an impressive rhetorical energy released, even when the argument does not fully convince.

> It seems a long way from Fenimore Cooper to Poe. But in fact it is only a step. Leatherstocking is the last instance of the integral, progressive, soul of the white man in America. In the last conjunction between Leatherstocking and Chingachgook we see the passing out into the darkness of the interim, as a seed falls into the dark interval of winter. What remains is the old tree withering and seething down to the crisis of winter-death, the great white race in America keenly disintegrating, seething back in electric decomposition, back to that crisis where the old soul, the old era, perishes in the denuded frame of man, and the first throb of a new year sets in.
> The process of the decomposition of the body after death is slow and mysterious, a life process of post-mortem activity.

... This is how man must bury his own dead self: in pang after pang of vital, explosive self-reduction, back to the elements.

... And in Poe, love is purely a frictional, destructive force. In him, the mystic, spontaneous self is replaced by the self-determined ego. He is a unit of will rather than a unit of being.

... If God is a great will, then the universe is a great machine, for the will is a fixed principle. But God is a mystery, from which creation mysteriously proceeds. So is the self a unit of creative mystery. But the will is the greatest of all control-principles, the greatest machine-principle.[11]

The machine-principle is equated with disintegration and set over against the living; on the other hand disintegration is part of the great *organic* cycle. Self-reduction (sensationalism) is vital, and also a process of decay opposed sharply to growth. It may perhaps be objected that this paradox is at least partly spurious, that we are being tricked by a ceaseless shifting between various senses of 'living'. The disintegration is living, we gather, in the sense that it contains and conceals life, as the pure death of winter conceals and prepares the way for spring; or again, in the sense that what is disintegrating is itself alive, though in the process of dying; or finally in the sense that the death process is violent and convulsive, and violence is a form of energy and energy of life. (There is certainly room for trickery in this last instance, for the energy in question may be a purposeful if vicious violence or the merely nervous and con-vulsive energy of an organism in its death-throes; and these are not living in anything like the same degree.) But all that matters for the student of Lawrence's fiction is the manifest impulse here *towards* the paradoxical, and the obvious bearing that the argument has upon *Women in Love* where, with greater cogency and by methods proper to art, the paradox of living disintegration is comprehensively articulated.

In *The Reality of Peace* Lawrence had shown himself even less inclined than he is in the essay on Poe to adopt a simplistic stance *vis-à-vis* disintegration.*

---

* Also relevant is a passage in the earlier essay, *Study of Thomas Hardy:*

Why does a snake horrify us, or even a newt? Why was Phillotson like a newt? What is it, in our life or in our feeling, to which a newt corresponds? Is it that life has the two sides, of growth and of decay, symbolized most acutely in our bodies by the semen and the excreta? Is it that the newt,

The wheat is put together by the pure activity of creation. It is the bread of pure creation I eat in the body. The fire of creation from out of the wheat passes into my blood, and what was put together in the pure grain now comes asunder, the fire mounts up into my blood, the watery mould washes back down my belly to the underearth. These are the two motions wherein we have our life. Is either a shame to me? Is it a pride to me that in my blood the fire flickers out of the wheaten bread I have partaken of, flickers up to further and higher creation? Then how shall it be a shame that from my blood exudes the bitter sweat of corruption on the journey back to dissolution; how shall it be a shame that in my consciousness appear the heavy marsh-flowers of the flux of putrescence, which have their natural roots in the slow stream of decomposition that flows for ever down my bowels?

There is a natural marsh in my belly, and there the snake is naturally at home. Shall he not crawl into my consciousness? Shall I kill him with sticks the moment he lifts his flattened head on my sight? Shall I kill him or pluck out the eye which sees him? None the less, he will swarm within the marsh.

Then let the serpent of living corruption take his place among us honourably.

We observe how easily and naturally in these discursive writings Lawrence moves between the concepts of dissolution, disintegration and corruption. These are all modes of what he calls in *The Crown*[12] the activity of departure, a *vital* reductive process that he images habitually in precisely those terms which he employed for the *mechanical* reductive process: 'frictional', 'disruptive', 'explosive', 'convulsive', 'electric', 'refracted', 'incandescent', 'phosphorescent'. We recall that in *Women in Love* it is not only Gerald and Gudrun to whom this language is relevant but Birkin also: his life-giving and disintegrative attack on the image of the moon is conceived of, in part, in just these terms.

The disposition to find a beauty and vitality in corruption was

---

the reptile, belong to the putrescent activity of life; the bird, the fish to the growth activity? Is it that the newt and the reptile are suggested to us through those sensations connected with excretion? And was Phillotson more or less connected with the decay activity of life? Was it his function to re-organize the life-excreta of the ages? At any rate, one can honour him, for he was true to himself.

scarcely novel of course; we have long recognized how much these notions had been in the air in the century before Lawrence began to write. ('What may be called the fascination of corruption penetrates in every touch of its exquisitely finished beauty', Pater wrote of a seventeenth-century head of the Medusa—attributed at that time to Leonardo —and the remark will serve as a representative utterance of 'The Romantic Agony'.) But there *is* novelty in the way Lawrence turns the tradition to account. In particular there is novelty in his habit of affirming demonic and paradisal values simultaneously: that is, in his endorsing the cult of corruption and at the same time judging it with all possible harshness—opposing to it a religion of pure creativeness, or an unambiguous vitalism. It is characteristic that in the passage I have just quoted from *The Reality of Peace* he should insist on the living value of impurity and putrescence and in the same breath celebrate the pure activity of creation. In *Women in Love*, needless to say, the effects are far more complex than this. Indeed Lawrence might seem to lay himself open there to just that charge he had brought against Dostoievsky: he seems at first glance to mix God and sadism, or creation and decomposition. Certainly he mixes two distinct traditions of Romanticism, the demonic and the organicist (or Wordsworthian), in very audacious ways. But I return to this topic later, and for the moment limit myself to the assertion that we will go hopelessly astray in our reading of the major fiction if we assume that, quite simply, Lawrence spoke for life and growth as against mechanism and the flux of corruption.

V Intensification-in-reduction

What Lawrence himself might well have called a 'double rhythm'
(the phrase comes from the revised essay on Poe) runs through a great
deal of the poetry of the Romantics. If the trance, the swoon, the
moment of self-destruction are thematically crucial in this poetry, that
is merely an obvious token of a persistent idiom of paradox; we observe
again and again that a rhythm of enhancement or intensification is
countered simultaneously by a rhythm of reduction. And though it is not
a matter susceptible to decisive proof, it is my conviction that the
paradox of living disintegration which Lawrence was so deeply engaged
with in the years in which he produced his finest fiction is ultimately
rooted in this characteristically Romantic ambiguity.

The dual rhythm whereby a dissolution of consciousness or being—
a process of reduction*—affects us at the same time as intensification
(a heightening, refining or rarifying) is so marked a feature of Romantic
poetry that it may well seem superfluous to illustrate it. Yet illustration
in some degree is necessary if my argument about the way Lawrence's
art was nourished from the past is to carry conviction. Here is one
relevant text:

* The natural association between the notions of flowing, melting and
reducing may be illustrated by the following passage from *The Prelude*,
Book VII (1805), though here it is not a dissolution of consciousness that
is being recorded:

> Oh, blank confusion! true epitome
> Of what the mighty City is herself
> To thousands upon thousands of her sons,
> Living amid the same perpetual whirl
> Of trivial objects, melted and reduced
> To one identity, by differences
> That have no law, no meaning, and no end— . . .

21

> Sound needed none,
> Nor any voice of joy; his spirit drank
> The spectacle: sensation, soul, and form,
> All melted into him; they swallowed up
> His animal being; in them did he live,
> And by them did he live; they were his life.[13]

In his recent book on *Wordsworth and The Artist's Vision* Alec King remarks, concerning this kind of experience:

> ... We know the superficial bodily response to music, the dance of muscle which may be no more than a faint rhythmic motion, and the half-consciousness of the rhythm of the heart-beat and of the lungs, to which the metronome rhythms of music are surely linked. Such shallow response corresponds to what Wordsworth called 'animal pleasure'. But when we listen to music deeply so that 'we are the music while the music lasts' our bodies get still, not because we leave them behind and enter the world of spirit, but because the full abundance, variety, subtlety of interfusing, and the resultant miracle of harmonizing such complexity, are such that overt movements of body are inconceivably clumsy and inappropriate. But the body is anything but non-existent; its nervous life is capable of extreme subtlety when it is released from the domination of its cruder surface behaviour. ...

In short, there is a sense in which the body dissolves and another sense in which it doesn't: the clumsiness of corporeality is suspended, yet the body is anything but non-existent. The word 'subtlety' here—'subtlety of interfusing', extreme subtlety'—has an appropriateness other than that intended; for it hints at the meaning 'tenuity' or 'rarity', without however involving a fatal commitment to the notion of disembodiment.

We see then why Wordsworth should resort so frequently to images of dissolution. The 'spectacle', in the lines under review, is ambiguously substantial-insubstantial; 'form' refers to the articulation or patterning of the given scene as it exists both within the mind and without.* At the

---

* In *Romantic Paradox: An Essay on the Poetry of Wordsworth* (Routledge and Kegan Paul, 1962) I have analysed the ambiguities of the Wordsworthian image in some detail, using as epigraph to the essay the equivocal statement from *The Prelude* (1805):

> ... I still
> At all times had a real solid world
> Of images about me ...[14]

moment of heightened consciousness one of the components of this ambiguous unity yields completely to the other; reality as solid substance gives way uncompromisingly to reality as experience. And Wordsworth dramatizes the process as much as anything via an equivocation in 'melted'. Sensation, soul and form melt as a tangible substance melts *away* into an intangible, but also as intangible substances melt *into* each other—as, say, vapour into vapour. The second of these readings confirms our commonsense assumption that the dissolving takes place wholly within the mind; in moments of intense consciousness such as this it is not, we know, the material world itself that melts! By means of the equivoque however Wordsworth contrives to makes a claim of just this extravagant kind, while yet seeming to deny it. So the objections of common-sense are circumvented, or muted.

Ambiguity of this sort is found on all sides in Romantic poetry. It is an ambiguity that most often registers itself as a confusion—sometimes enriching, sometimes disabling—between a dissolving of *consciousness* and the *content* of consciousness, or sensations and objects sensed, or images and things imaged. In *Tintern Abbey*, for instance, these dubieties are apparent wherever we turn.

> . . . that blessed mood,
> In which the burthen of the mystery,
> In which the heavy and the weary weight
> Of all this unintelligible world,
> Is lightened . . .

Is the weary weight a spiritual weight only (the burthen of the *mystery*) or is it also a physical weight, a weight that is lightened in the sense that the solid forms of nature dissolve, or are sublimated, into inward ones, until finally all sense of materiality, either in the body or outwardly, leaves us and we see directly into the life of things? That equation 'dissolve, *or* are sublimated' is not an unjustified imposition of meaning; it is there in the text. For, if the poem is a good deal concerned with dissolution—the dissolving of the substantial outward world into a tenuous inwardness—it is equally concerned to plot a process of sublimation: 'And passing even into my purer mind', 'Of aspect more sublime', 'The coarser pleasures of my boyish days, And their glad animal movements all gone by'. And the one process is indirectly equated with the other: the further the dissolution goes, the more sublime the vision—'a sense *sublime* Of something far more deeply *interfused*'. If the sense is sublime or sublimated so is whatever the sense is *of*, and if the something is interfused so is the sense: we tend to assume this because

23

sublimation and fusion are both modes of dissolution and because the poem has taught us that thought and things interpenetrate. In short, the commonsense view that substances necessarily remain distinct from each other (round ocean, living air, blue sky, the mind of man and so on) is supplemented by the opposite view: at a deeper level, it is implied, the separateness of things is of less account than their unity, and Reality is not so much a manifold as a process, a flux. At this level all things are fused, all things flow. (Hence 'a *motion* and a spirit', 'impels', 'rolls through'.)

The dual rhythm to which I have referred is not of course established in Romantic poetry only through images of dissolution.

> . . . that serene and blessed mood,
> In which the affections gently lead us on,—
> Until, the breath of this corporeal frame
> And even the motion of our human blood
> Almost suspended, we are laid asleep
> In body, and become a living soul.

This language would seem almost as appropriate if what was in question was the oncoming of death; and this appropriateness appears the more significant if we take into account the intermittent if subdued note of world-weariness in the poem ('all/The dreary intercourse of daily life') and the tentative echoes of *Hamlet*.* Here are resonances that contribute materially to our haunting sense that throughout the poem it is not only an intensification but also a deprivation or reduction of life that is being recorded.

In the poetry of Keats analogous dubieties are common:

> Into her dream he melted, as the rose
> Blendeth its odour with the violet,—
> Solution sweet.

He melts into her dream as something intangible might (an odour), passing into it imperceptibly; that is, 'solution' means fusion. But 'solution' also hints at the sense dis-solution (and for that matter, resolution). In other words it implies, conceivably, that the melting is a 'liquefaction through heat' (an obsolete sense) or, more certainly, a 'liquefaction by means of a fluid or solvent'; at all events what is in question is a melting in sexual consummation. In short, the equivocations allow Keats to have it both ways; the dissolution is at once chaste

* With 'the burthen . . . the weary weight' and 'the fretful stir/ Unprofitable' compare 'How weary, stale, flat, and unprofitable' and 'To grunt and sweat under a weary life'.

and carnal. Moreover, and more to the point, we respond at one and the same time to a rhythm of reduction (there is a loss of identity, whether the melting-and-fusing is that of a solid or of something tenuous) and of intensification (the moment of dissolution is climactic; narrative and syntax both affirm it). The one rhythm cannot be dissociated from the other; it is a process of intensification-*in*-reduction.

There is another instance of this sort of double-talk in a celebrated passage in Book One of *Endymion*.

> Wherein lies happiness ? In that which becks
> Our ready minds to fellowship divine,
> A fellowship with essence; till we shine,
> Full alchemiz'd, and free of space . . .
> . . . . But there are
> Richer entanglements, enthralments far
> More self-destroying, leading, by degrees,
> To the chief intensity; the crown of these
> Is made of love and friendship, and sits high
> Upon the forehead of humanity.
> All its more ponderous and bulky worth
> Is friendship, whence there ever issues forth
> A steady splendour; but at the tip-top,
> There hangs by unseen film, an orbed drop
> Of light, and that is love: its influence,
> Thrown in our eyes, genders a novel sense,
> At which we start and fret; till in the end,
> Melting into its radiance, we blend,
> Mingle, and so become a part of it,—
> Nor with aught else can our souls interknit
> So wingedly: when we combine therewith,
> Life's self is nourish'd by its proper pith,
> And we are nurtured like a pelican brood.
> Aye, so delicious is the unsating food . . .

The lines at the beginning are not about aesthetic rapture in any transcendental sense*; nevertheless the emphasis here, and throughout the first half of Endymion's discourse, is all on sublimation, or dissolution in the sense of disembodiment; and human love is conceived of at first in the same rarified terms. But we don't stay at that level; there is a change of tenor, and love becomes a 'delicious . . . unsating food', an 'ardent listlessness'. The transition is a little awkward and would have

---

* See 'The Meaning of "Fellowship with essence" in *Endymion*', Newell F. Ford, *PMLA* (1947). Ford demonstrates convincingly that essence is a synonym for the aesthetic object (a rose leaf or lover or love itself) and that fellowship denotes a pleasurable 'oneness' with it.

been a good deal more so but for the ingenious juggling with metaphors of melting, blending and mingling—if 'juggling' does not suggest an art more contrived than this in fact is. Take the image of melting at its face value and one is still in the tenuous region of imaginative rapture and chastity, for it is not heat that is denoted by the word 'radiance' but light; the melting is apparently not a liquefaction but a merging of vapour into vapour, spirit into spirit. On the other hand, given the context—a discussion of love—and given the time-worn association of melting and the heat of desire, the phrase 'melting into its radiance' can scarcely fail to have erotic implications, and if we respond to these we are prepared to some extent for the ensuing celebration of romantic passion. In effect the ambiguity glosses over the whole problem of fusing idealism and sensuality in love (as the denouement at the end of Book Four does too); the ancient quarrel between them is resolved by an equivocation before it can fairly declare itself.

It is not surprising that after *Endymion* Keats should have gone on to write both *The Eve of St. Agnes and Isabella*, the one all 'wormy circumstance' and the other a delicious 'wakeful swoon'; for the too-easy accommodation of idealism to sensuality in *Endymion* entails in effect their partial dissociation (the confrontation is more apparent than real) and this in turn entails the dissociating of idealism and *corruption*. In *Lamia*, by contrast, it is precisely the perception of an ironic relation between the corruptive and the ideal that provides Keats with his theme. It was about this time that he annotated a section of Burton's *Anatomy of Melancholy* to the following effect:

> Here is the old plague-spot: the pestilence, the raw scrofula. I mean there is nothing disgraces me in my own eyes so much as being one of a race of eyes, nose and mouth beings in a planet called the earth who all from Plato to Wesley have always mingled goatish, winnyish, lustful love with the abstract adoration of the deity. I don't understand Greek—is the Love of God and the Love of women expressed by the same word in Greek? I hope my little mind is wrong—if not I could—Has Plato separated these loves? Ha! I see how they endeavour to divide—but there appears to be a horrid relationship.

This evolving sense of an inner logic that relates the ideal to the carnal, or imagination to corruption, is articulated with special poignancy in *Ode to a Nightingale*. Lawrence, we have noticed, remarked of Keats's poetry:

. . . the body can still be *felt* dissolving in waves of successive death.

The word dissolving makes it probable that it was the Nightingale ode Lawrence had above all in mind, so it is worth remarking that this poem develops the theme of dissolution with an ambivalent subtlety directly prophetic of Lawrence's own.

Fade far away, dissolve, and quite forget . . .

—either quite forget in death or, less absolutely, through a transcending of everyday consciousness.

> I cannot see what flowers are at my feet,
> Nor what soft incense hangs upon the boughs,
> But, in embalmed darkness, guess each sweet . . .

The fading into darkness brings an access of being, a sharpening of imaginative perception; but it is an approach also to the last insensitivity. The fading violets are covered up in leaves and the covering up takes place in embalmed darkness—'embalmed' suggesting both scented, or balmy, and the art of the embalmer. But there is little point in teasing out these indirections of meaning; clearly the fading is a fading both in visionary rapture and in the ecstasy of death. The poem is about the need to die if we are to live imaginatively—and, equally, about the need to resist this dying. The ambivalence is as it were built in to the radical image. Keats's actualizing of this ambivalence is at the same time a discovering of his theme. But there is a further sense of dissolution present in the poem, as Lawrence's comment by implication recognizes. I refer to the sense, 'decomposition'. The more the poet dwells longingly on the notion of painless dissolution the more we are reminded of what in real life dissolution would be likely to entail; and this is not only true of Stanza Three.

> Where palsy shakes a few, sad, last gray hairs,
> Where youth grows pale, and spectre-thin, and dies . . .

Dissolution is a *physical* fact in the poem, however much the poet wills it to be something else. What is entailed in Lawrence's comment is a recognition that the poem does not in fact keep these two kinds of dissolution—decomposition and disembodiment—distinct. The body can be felt dissolving not only because (in Lawrence's view) the body is at any rate tangibly there as it isn't in the work of Shelley, but because the very language in which Keats wills his easeful dissolution puts us in mind of the other, uglier kind of dissolution; the two meanings inevitably

27

suggest or attract each other as well as being, inevitably, foils to each other.

In Lawrence's work this particular kind of tension is common, as in the chapter concerned with Mr Crich's dying and denial of dying in *Women in Love*—where, incidentally, images of dissolution proliferate. So too Gerald's 'pure and exalted activity' as a mine-owner ('He had converted the industry into a new and terrible purity') has for corollary his implication in 'abhorent mysteries' (I have in mind the chapter 'Rabbit', which immediately succeeds the chapter 'The Industrial Magnate') and his patent drift towards death. But I have touched on this correlating of decay and abstraction in *Women in Love* already. Indeed this discussion of Lawrence's Romantic affiliations is bound to turn in on itself to some extent.* Inevitably one will revert from time to time to the starting-point: the tendency of images of dissolution to polarise, pointing to possibilities both of disembodiment and decay, ecstasy and reduction.

And in one sense the following section likewise turns back to the beginning.

* The self-destructiveness of the Romantic imagination has of course been a good deal commented on. What I have called intensification-in-reduction is E. H. Davidson's subject, for instance, in his *Poe: A Critical Study* (1964), when he notes how 'the imagination destroying itself in the very act of creation' is a 'pervasive element' both in Poe's art and in Romantic literature generally. 'One of the most fascinating aspects of the Romantic mind was that it wore itself out or even destroyed its own imaginative powers . . . Poe belonged to the company of Shelley, Coleridge, Pushkin, Verlaine, and others too numerous to mention' (pp. 45–7). It should perhaps be added here that Poe's considerable indebtedness to Shelley has been stressed by Julia Power in her *Shelley in America* (1964).

VI 'Dissolves, diffuses, dissipates'

It is partly because ambiguities about fading, melting and fusing are so common in the work of Wordsworth, Keats and Shelley,* and because their pervasive doubleness of vision has come to seem so natural to us, that Coleridge's famous statement about the Secondary Imagina-

* The pejorative use of 'dissolves' in the following passage goes a long way towards explaining why ambiguities about dissolution are not to be found in the work of Blake:

> Nature has no Outline, but Imagination has . . . Nature has no Supernatural, and dissolves: Imagination is Eternity.
> (*The Ghost of Abel*)

Admittedly there is a sense in which the 'outline' in Blake's poetry, and this applies especially to the Prophetic writings, is anything but sharp, and the appropriateness of the word 'dissolves' in the following comment by Yeats is undeniable:

> Things we have to give in *succession* in our explanatory prose are set forth *simultaneously* in Blake's verse. From this arises the greater part of the obscurity of the symbolic books. The surface is perpetually, as it were, giving way before one, and revealing another surface below it, and that again dissolves when we try to study it.
> (*The Works of William Blake*, Ellis & Yeats, 3 vols, London, 1893, p. 287).

It remains true however that images of melting etc. are not thematically central in the poetry of Blake and I think we are justified in connecting this fact with the doctrine he formulates in *The Ghost of Abel* and elsewhere. (See the *Descriptive Catalogue* and the marginalia to Reynolds' *Discourses*, *William Blake's Prophetic Writings*, ed. Sloss & Wallis, Oxford, repr. 1957, Vol. II, especially pp. 294 and 326.)

tion is rarely interpreted today in the sense that seems, logically, most appropriate. Or, to make the point the other way round, when Coleridge declares that the Secondary Imagination 'dissolves, diffuses, dissipates', readers readily discover in his language the kind of ambiguous significance they would be likely to find in a corresponding language-pattern in Romantic *poetry*, although, in so far as their sense of logic is appealed to, they are positively discouraged from doing so. Here is the passage in full:

> The IMAGINATION then, I consider either as primary, or secondary. The primary IMAGINATION I hold to be the living Power and prime Agent of all human Perception, and as a repetition in the finite mind of the eternal act of creation in the infinite I AM. The secondary Imagination I consider as an echo of the former, co-existing with the conscious will, yet still as identical with the primary in the *kind* of its agency, and differing only in *degree*, and in the *mode* of its operation. It dissolves, diffuses, dissipates, in order to recreate; or where this process is rendered impossible, yet still at all events it struggles to idealize and to unify. It is essentially *vital*, even as all objects (*as* objects) are essentially fixed and dead.

The cumulative effect of the three verbs is such as to draw attention to the possible duality or dubiety of meaning in 'dissolves' that I have already remarked on: the word can have the force both of 'liquefies-and-disperses' and of 'disperses-without-liquefying, as in the melting and dispersal of a mist'. There appears to be nothing in the immediate linguistic context to prevent the former meaning from asserting itself, and indeed, as I have said, the juxtaposition of the three verbs in fact tends to enforce it.

To begin with, a possible sense of diffuses is 'pours out as a *fluid* with wide dispersal', and this reinforces the meaning 'liquefies', already there potentially in 'dissolves'. Moreover this mutual assimilating of the senses of dissolves and diffuses, so that they seem to refer to a single operation of liquefying-and-blending, is facilitated by the fact that dissolves can refer not only to the process of reducing *to* a liquid but to the process of liquefying by immersion *in* a liquid: i.e. the diffusion of molecules of a solid or gas in a liquid so that they become indistinguishable from it. Then again, dissipates can mean not only 'disperses' but 'dissolves utterly', so that the addition of this third verb leaves us with the original ambiguity still on our hands: that is, leaves us as much in doubt as ever whether what is dissolved is a vapour or a solid.

In a valuable discussion of what Coleridge meant by his famous pronouncement Nicholas Brooke remarks:[15]

> The verbs [dissolves, diffuses, dissipates] have been assumed to refer to 'objects' because that is the only noun in the rest of Coleridge's paragraph to which they could apply. That, as I understand them, is the sense Richards and Willey give the phrase: but I find it very unsatisfactory. The theory of perception, of imaginative activity, that I have discussed, is of a coalescence between self and object in which *both* must be assumed to exist. In that theory one cannot speak of 'dissolving' the object, because that reduces the object to a phantom, something which does not exist. The confusion is kept alive in the popularity of chemical metaphors for imagination: you can 'dissolve' iron (by melting it) and the resultant liquid will 'mix' with some other liquids apparently unlike it in kind. But this process is not much use to poetry: it may be that in thinking of iron as cold and hard we are mistaking its nature; but until we understand it better, those remain its perceived, imaginative qualities . . . What is dissolved, diffused and dissipated is the *deadness* of dull response, the attenuated cloud that obscures perception; and it is also the *fixity* of relationships in time and space—the fixity of fact that keeps irons in the grate, or for John Gabriel Borkman locked in mountains of stone, utterly distinct from the hearts of men. It is that apparently fixed disjunction which is dissolved: the iron-ness of iron is not changed at all.*

Illuminating though this is up to a point, one is left with a doubt whether the usual reading is actually as groundless as Professor Brooke suggests. Isn't there a sense in which, if the attenuated cloud obscuring perception is dissipated, the substantial and all-too-familiar world of perceived objects is dissipated too ? That is, there can be no genuine dissipating of the cloud which is not at the same time a dissipating of the objects

---

* Professor Brooke argues that the 'objects' of which Coleridge speaks—'objects (*as* objects) are essentially fixed and dead'—are not 'the "inanimate, cold word" of the Primary Imagination', as Basil Willey suggested, since 'the Primary Imagination has been defined as a *living* power, whose function is *creative*'; the objects are rather 'objects, *as* objects-as-opposed-to-subjects'. That is, they are abstractions. One can think about them, but one cannot *know* them, since knowing involves a creative coalescence of subject and object.

perceived *through* the cloud. To the extent that the experience of dissolution is emotionally real, the objects themselves really dissolve. After all, Coleridge's word 'recreate' ('dissolves, diffuses, dissipates, in order to recreate') itself implies that the dissolution is radical, because it implies a starting again from the beginning; and our disposition to assume that dissolves means 'dissolves corporeally' is an oblique tribute to this fact. In short, though it will readily be granted that objects of perception are indissoluble—they exist in their own right, are not phantoms—it must be conceded that the direct opposite of this proposition is equally true: there is a sense, which the emotions acknowledge in despite of reason, in which the iron-ness of iron *is* changed by the imagination. And it is the ambiguity latent in his images of dissolution that allows Coleridge to articulate this antinomy without at the same time flagrantly affronting commonsense.

The verses of Sir John Davies quoted at the end of Chapter XIV of the *Biographia* serve to confirm this reading, I think:

> Doubtless this could not be, but that she turns
> Bodies to spirit by sublimation strange,
> As fire converts to fire the things it burns,
> As we our food into our nature change.

(And so on.) This quotation follows directly upon Coleridge's famous list of fusions: 'of sameness, with difference; of the general, with the concrete; the idea, with the image', etc.—a list in which, as Professor Brooke remarks, no fusion is of object and object. It is all the more significant therefore that the 'sublimation strange' that Davies is concerned with should be, apparently, a metamorphosis of material substance ('As fire converts to fire the things it burns'). What tends to be implied by the list of fusions is that the given world is indissoluble; what on the contrary is indicated by Davies' verses is that the corporeal habitually yields to or dissolves into the incorporeal. And, as I began by suggesting, far from surprising us, this is a kind of equivocation we go half-way to meet. We very readily believe that body both can and cannot be sublimated into spirit. And we easily assume that a dissolving which is also a diffusing and dissipating is a dissolving of the vaporous *and* the solid, or more probably, and however paradoxically, a dissolving of the vaporous-solid; for that is what our reading of Romantic poetry has so thoroughly *taught* us to assume.

The imaginative process, in short, is a corporeal-spiritual process of reduction.

VII Flux and irony

There is no sharp distinction to be drawn between imagery of dissolution and imagery of flux in the poetry of the Romantics, and the former no less than the latter is a token of their preoccupation with process or becoming, and of their assumption that experience is an unbroken flow. The lover or the visionary soul fades, fuses, lapses, dissolves, melts without effort, imperceptibly perhaps, from one state of being to another ('the affections gently lead us on') so that a given phase of consciousness cannot be abruptly distinguished from the phase from which it emerged. There is scope here for self-deception on the poet's part, as well as for subtlety and richness. (The passage quoted above from *Endymion* is a case in point; indeed the entire tradition of spiritualized eroticism that leads from Keats and Shelley, through Rossetti, to the early Yeats is relevant.) And also there is scope for irony, whether availed of or not. For (by implication) Romantic poetry is constantly revealing, or half-revealing, the essential inward similarity of experiences that are nevertheless and in crucial ways dis-similar.

Lawrence exploited this situation to the full. It is his practice to play off against each other *kinds* of dissolving or melting or swooning with a degree of sophistication that has rarely been acknowledged. Representative is that episode in *Women in Love* where Gerald comes to Gudrun's bedroom, having stolen into the Brangwen house in the middle of the night.

> Into her he poured all his pent-up darkness and
> corrosive death, and he was whole again. . . .
>
> He felt himself dissolving and sinking to rest in
> the bath of her living strength. . . .

It has been remarked that Gerald does obeisance here to a *magna mater* figure.[16] This is true enough in itself, but *by* itself it is misleading. For if the satisfaction Gerald enjoys is that of a child, or of the infant bathed in the womb, it is also, and without any shadow of qualification or criticism, that of a man.

> All his veins, that were murdered and lacerated, healed softly as life came pulsing in, stealing invisibly into him as if it were the all-powerful effluence of the sun. His blood, which seemed to have been drawn back into death, came ebbing on the return, surely, beautifully, powerfully.

There is no denying that final resonance; it has the richness, strength and confidence appropriate to fully adult satisfaction.

> He was a man again, strong and rounded. And he was a child, so soothed and restored and full of gratitude.

The two declarations are laid side by side, and there is no alternative but to keep them in mind simultaneously. For no attempt is made to reconcile them. Gerald establishes communion with profound sources of vitality, and is made whole; but also the wholeness he achieves is illusory. The strategy here is characteristic of the novel throughout, and it makes great demands on the reader's responsiveness. The process of dissolution, the lapsing of consciousness and the letting in of power from the unknown—a flood of power from the unconquerable sun—is a redemptive process, and the transmutation of Gerald's corrosive sexuality into a 'lovely creative warmth' enforces this truth irresistably. (It is a truth further enforced by the contrast here between Gerald and Gudrun. Lacking his capacity for dissolution, she lies staring into the darkness in anguished self-consciousness.) On the other hand Gerald's sexuality *is* reductive, and our sense of this is confirmed by the way the process of dissolution to which he commits himself is at the same time a resolving out of his essential manhood, an activity of fusion and immersion which the novel has already taught us abundantly to suspect.

This is an art more sophisticated than we are likely to find in the work of the Romantics, yet the material for these ironic juxtapositions was already lying there in Romantic poetry, ready to hand. It is as though in this episode Lawrence were envisaging, and dramatizing, the potential self-destructiveness and infantalism which he claimed again and again to be characteristic of the Romantic, and superimposing this envisaged condition upon a perception of Romantic joy and plenitude. And the latent ambiguity in the imagery he inherited makes it possible for him to do so with unique ironic power.

He is particularly inclined to direct this power upon the manifold relations of the sacred and profane, on visionary exaltations and erotic ecstasies, and one thinks how variously and suggestively these themes bear upon each other in the poetry of the Romantics, how for instance Wordsworth's visionary rapture looks forward to the voluptuousness of Keats. There is a sense for example in which sex is absent from *Tintern Abbey* and another sense in which it isn't. It is not really surprising that Keats should have caught up the phrase 'wild ecstasies' into a highly erotic context in *Ode on a Grecian Urn*. For Wordsworth's characteristic imagery prepared the way for, and encouraged, precisely that marriage between sensuousness and sexuality which his own predominant interests, and perhaps his anxieties, ruled out. The frequent use he makes of images of dissolution and sublimation, the confusion between a dissolving of consciousness and a dissolving of the substantial world of sense, the possibility of a confusion between surrendering to the sleep of vision and surrendering to the sleep of death: all this was of the first importance. The transition from the Wordsworthian trance to the Keatsian swoon, from fading in reverie to fading in passion, or into the last oblivion of death, is clearly not a difficult one. Indeed the fact that the poetry of Keats and Shelley should live in such significant proximity to the poetry of Wordsworth—so patently akin and so strikingly different—is itself a fine instance of the sort of ironic juxtaposition in which *Women in Love* abounds. It is partly for this reason indeed that *Women in Love* is of such importance in modern literature; here for the first time English Romanticism becomes fully self-conscious.

VIII The downward rhythm

I want to focus attention now on a single recurrent metaphor in *Women in Love* by way of illustrating my general argument that the manner in which the imagery of dissolution is articulated throughout reflects large ambiguous rhythms in Romantic poetry. (I use the terms metaphor and image interchangeably and, where relevant, in such a way as not to exclude altogether the further connotation, 'concept'. For the distinction between concept and image cannot be a sharp one where Lawrence is concerned; his thinking is profoundly analogical.)

So intricately does the imagery ramify that if we choose to call the novel as a whole an extended metaphor then we may say, indifferently, that that metaphor is dissolution *or* disintegration *or* corruption. Wherever we break into the text for the purpose of critical comment we are likely to be led on, via trains of association, to a consideration of the major patterns of metaphor; if the object is to demonstrate the extensive reverberation of meaning, it does not matter greatly where we begin. I choose the following from the chapter 'Flitting' because it might seem to do so little to support my case:

> But the passion of gratitude with which he received her into his soul, the extreme, unthinkable gladness of knowing himself living and fit to unite with her, he, who was so nearly dead, who was so near to being gone with the rest of his race down the slope of mechanical death, could never be understood by her. He worshipped her as age worships youth, he gloried in her because, in his one grain of faith, he was young as she, he was her proper mate. This marriage with her was his resurrection and his life.

In his book *Double Measure* George Ford devotes a number of paragraphs to that image of the death-slope. He shows how it crops up in the essay

The Crown and in a war-time letter: 'I dance with joy when I see him rushing down the Gadarene slope of the war'. He remarks:

> For Lawrence's purposes in 1916–17, the story of the
> Gadarene swine was richly suggestive . . .
> Here was an image suggesting the combination of
> swinish sensual corruption with a herd madness, an in-
> explicable propulsion towards self-destruction.

And then he quotes the passage about going down the slope of mechanical death. His commentary is relevant of course, and yet because it stops where it does it deprives the image of some of its resonance, for this is only one of hundreds of images in the novel concerned with downward movement, and our response to it is inevitably affected by our response to all those that have gone before. There is this for example:

> It was the strange mystery of his life-motion, there, at the
> back of the thighs, *down* the flanks. It was a strange reality
> of his being, the very stuff of being, there in the straight
> *downflow* of the thighs. . . .
>   After a lapse of stillness, after the rivers of strange dark
> fluid richness had passed over her, flooding, carrying away
> her mind and flooding *down* her spine and *down* her
> knees . . .
> Her arms closed around him again, her hands spread upon
> his shoulders, moving slowly there, moving slowly on his
> back, *down* his back slowly, with a strange recurrent,
> rhythmic motion, yet moving slowly *down*. . . . And she did
> not speak, but only pressed her hands firmer *down* upon
> the source of darkness in him.

Commentators have written off this episode with monotonous unanimity; in fact however something very like it was a necessity in the novel. What has disturbed some critics is the similarity of certain phrases to the phrasing in that passage about the African fetish, in 'Moony': we cannot but compare 'deeper than the phallic source', 'deeper, further in mystery than the phallic source' with 'How far, in their inverted culture, had these West Africans gone beyond phallic knowledge?' and 'This was far beyond any phallic knowledge, sensual subtle realities far beyond the scope of phallic investigation'. This oblique analogy, in the opinion of the critics in question, is evidence of a spiritual sickness in Birkin and Ursula, and particularly Birkin (who yet, they claim, is clearly meant to embody a norm) and evidence therefore of a failure in artistic control. Yet the passage in 'Excurse' positively *invites* comparison with the earlier one, as it also does, for that matter, with that passage in 'Water Party' about the river of dissolution. 'Rivers of strange dark fluid richness' pass over Ursula, and there is little doubt to which of the two rivers distinguished earlier by Birkin these more nearly correspond. At the very moment when the lovers release in themselves a full flow of life we are encouraged to note the analogy with the flux of corruption, and even, indeed, with the awful African process. But if the interpretation of the novel I have been offering is sound then all this is as we should expect; in other words we ought not to be surprised to find that once again life is affirmed in reduction. 'Down his back slowly . . . moving slowly down': it is only another instance of that positive-reductive process of dissolution to which the novel as a whole is one comprehensive tribute.*

* It is important to distinguish here between Lawrence's art and his 'doctrine', as expressed in conversation, letters or essays; and in this connexion I would quote the following passage from Frederick Carter's *D. H. Lawrence and the Body Mystical*. Carter focusses attention very effectively on the importance of downward movement in Lawrence's thought and imagination; on the other hand what he says cannot be applied to *Women in Love* without large reservations, for he assumes—whether on the basis of certain of the discursive writings or of personal discussion or of a too-casual reading of the fiction is not clear—that downward movement held for Lawrence a single, positive value:

> Then, too, he did not like the idea of 'ascent' or 'uplift'. What he wanted was not conquest by upward striving. It could improve nothing, for it already had gone on beyond its measure. We have too much of the head—of the cerebral nowadays. We need to get back to foundations. He declared for the great descent, for no more Logos, no more brain-stirring, but a new age with a downward return to the great dark centres, past the diaphragm and the navel, where was to be found the throne of power and the sceptre of rule. . . .
> . . . Heaven, he felt, must be dull—pathetically so—a place to escape from. In the descent lay the real splendour, in that down-pressing life which sought generation and centred itself below the midriff—a movement that joyed in the body. He would hail Man who broke from heaven and made the world; a Lucifer who separated, declaring that his multitudinous children should build towers to storm the skies. Aye, who would have daughters fair enough to distract the Angels from their abstract joys of contemplation towards the Godhead and bring them plunging down.

Here are some further contexts in which the image of downward movement occurs:

> She hated him in a despair that shattered her and broke her down, so that she suffered sheer dissolution like a corpse, and was unconscious of every thing save the horrible sickness of dissolution that was taking place within her, body and soul.[17]
>
> Then swiftly, in a flame that drenched down her body like fluid lightning and gave her a perfect, unutterable consummation, unutterable satisfaction, she brought down the ball of jewel stone with all her force, crash on his head.[18]
>
> After all, when one was fulfilled, one was happiest in falling into death, as a bitter fruit plunges in its ripeness downwards.[19]
>
> There is a long way we can travel, after the death-break; after that point when the soul in intense suffering breaks, breaks away from its organic hold like a leaf that falls. We fall from the connexion with life and hope, we lapse from pure integral being, from creation and liberty, and we fall into the long, long African process of purely sensual understanding, knowledge in the mystery of dissolution.[20]
>
> 'I suppose we want the same,' said Birkin. 'Only we want to take a quick jump downwards, in a sort of ecstasy—and he ebbs with the stream, the sewer stream.'[21]
>
> It was an unbroken will reacting against her unbroken will in a myriad subtle thrills of reduction, the last subtle activities of analysis and breaking down . . .[22]
>
> There was only the inner, individual darkness, sensation within the ego, the obscene religious mystery of ultimate reduction, the mystic frictional activities of diabolic reducing down, disintegrating the vital organic body of life.[23]

It might seem from these examples that the instances in which the downward movement is negative far outnumber those in which it is positive. But in fact this is not so, for I have quoted only those instances where the reference to falling or declining is particularly obvious. In the novel itself images of this kind modulate insensibly into a host of others that merely *hint* at downward movement.

Consider for a moment the recurrence of the word 'lapse'. Here are six instances out of many.

> 'You've got to *lapse out* before you can know what sensual reality is, lapse into unknowingness, and give up your

volition. You've got to do it. You've got to learn not-to-be, before you can come into being.'[24]

When the stream of synthetic creation *lapses*, we find ourselves part of the inverse process, the blood of destructive creation.[25]

Thousands of years ago, that which was imminent in himself must have taken place in these Africans: the goodness, the holiness, the desire for creation and productive happiness must have *lapsed*, leaving the single impulse for knowledge in one sort, mindless progressive knowledge through the senses, knowledge arrested and ending in the senses, mystic knowledge in disintegration and dissolution, knowledge such as the beetles have, which live purely within the world of corruption and cold dissolution. This was why her face looked like a beetle's: this was why the Egyptians worshipped the ball-rolling scarab: because of the principle of knowledge in dissolution and corruption.[26]

There is a long way we can travel, after the death-break: after that point when the soul in intense suffering breaks, breaks away from its organic hold like a leaf that falls. We fall from the connexion with life and hope, we *lapse* from pure-integral being, from creation and liberty, and we fall into the long, long African process of purely sensual understanding, knowledge in the mystery of dissolution.[27]

And they both felt the subterranean desire to let go, to fling away everything and *lapse* into a sheer unrestraint, brutal and licentious.[28]

The sense of the awfulness of riches that could never be impaired flooded her mind like a swoon, a death in most marvellous possession, mystic-sure. She possessed him so utterly and intolerably that she herself *lapsed out*.[29]

To lapse is to 'fall, decline, fall into decay' and also to 'glide, flow, glide past, pass away'; and these meanings easily entail or attract to themselves the meanings 'collapse', disintegrate, fall away, swoon, melt down, dissolve, be reduced' and so on. Nowhere in *Women in Love* is there an explicit play upon the various senses of lapse, yet the passages quoted show how easy is the transition in Lawrence's mind between lapsing in the sense of gliding or flowing, lapsing as a downward, falling movement, either creative or destructive, lapsing as the passing of time and lapsing as swooning, a dissolving or flooding away of consciousness.

In the third passage, though corruption is imaged as a beetle-rot and though the metaphor of a flux is missing, the language is of a kind that would make a transition to the missing metaphor easy. Lapse in this context means fall into decay rather than glide or flow; yet this alternative sense is clearly within reach, for 'progressive', 'long way', 'process' and 'dissolution' indicate that Lawrence's meaning could easily have been imaged in terms of a stream—a *flux* of corruption rather than a dry decay and disintegration.* It is no accident that Ursula's swoon— 'carrying away her mind', 'she herself lapsed out'—should be associated both with a flood and with a downward movement: 'flooding down her spine', 'down his back slowly', 'at the back and base of the loins'. Nor is it an accident that in Birkin's reflections on the African way the dissolving of mental consciousness ('mindless progressive knowledge', 'mystic knowledge in dissolution') should be associated not only with the downward movement of the leaf but with the passage or lapse of time.

In short, images of lapsing, streaming, falling and dissolving are so deviously and closely related in the novel's shifting linguistic contexts that any given use of one of the images is likely to entail the others, if only in a shadowy way; and any use where the context imposes on the image a predominantly pejorative or negative sense is apt to call to mind the possible *positive* sense, with the result that every usage is charged with either concealed or manifest tension.

And so with the image of the death-slope which I began by considering. This is an instance where the negative force of a reductive image is as extreme as it is anywhere in the novel. And yet even here we distort slightly when we consider it out of its total context; we deprive it of a certain vibrancy, attribute to it an absolute finality, and a flatness, which in its setting it doesn't have. For in this novel *any* image of dissolution or reduction, for the reasons just given, hints at possibilities of self-qualification, sets up at least a slight tremor of expectancy or doubt. And often the concealed impulse to qualify is quite as powerful as the overt impulse to affirm.

It is the vigour and persistence of this impulse to qualify that so distinguishes Lawrence from the great Romantics. Though the concern with activities of self-destruction and dissolution which he and they share affirms the close familial tie, the distance between them can often seem immense. Lawrence's phrasing can remind us quite close of Shelley's:

* Outside the context of this novel images of dry decay and flux are in fact brought together explicitly. See for instance the essay *The Return Journey*, from *Twilight in Italy*: 'And it seemed here, here in this holiday-place, was the quick of the disintegration, the dry-rot, in this dry, friable flux of people backwards and forwards on the edge of the lake . . .'

Sister of her whose footsteps pave the world
With loveliness—more fair than aught but her,
Whose shadow thou art—lift thine eyes on me.'
I lifted them: the overpowering light
Of that immortal shape was shadowed o'er
By love; which, from his soft and flowing limbs,
And passion-parted lips, and keen, faint eyes,
Steamed forth like vaporous fire; an atmosphere
Which wrapped me in its all-dissolving power,
As the warm aether of the morning sun
Wraps ere it drinks some cloud of wandering dew.
I saw not, heard not, moved not, only felt
His presence flow and mingle through my blood
Till it became his life, and his grew mine . . . .

This points forward clearly enough; we have every right to speak here of a tradition. On the other hand there is, in this passage from *Prometheus Unbound*, no qualifying irony, nothing witheld. (This is not in any sense a value judgment. Besides, it is not as though *Prometheus* were deficient in irony as a whole; if 'ecstasy', 'passion', the given mode of dissolution, is rarely in itself a theme for irony, there is a good deal else that is.) Panthea's religio-sexual joy is proposed as self-validating, whereas in *Women in Love* the life-value of a moment of equivalent intensity would nearly always be a matter for doubt. Indeed it is a common complaint that the erotic swoonings of the two pairs of lovers can only be distinguished with great difficulty, and sometimes not at all. But the difficulty is precisely the point. In any case, in assimilating the life-flow to the death-flow Lawrence at the same time distinguishes between them with a subtle, unflagging precision.

But before I go on to supply further evidence in support of this claim I want to say something about *The Rainbow*. This novel clearly represents an earlier stage in the articulation of those paradoxical 'convictions' which I have been considering. Again and again we can watch Lawrence feeling his way towards the audacious double-talk of *Women in Love* but achieving, instead, an effect of uneasy equivocation. His art hasn't always as yet the kind of flexibility that makes it possible for him to be self-contradictory without seeming to be *merely* self-contradictory. He seems concerned to say, from time to time, that corruption, violence, bestiality, 'all the shameful things of the body'[30] are both degrading and life-enhancing; but he only half-says it, and the result, particularly in the sequences involving Ursula and Skrebensky, is a certain disorganization—often trivial enough, but sometimes serious.

Part Two
The Activity of Departure

'And departure is the opposite equivalent
of coming together; decay, corruption, destruction,
breaking down is the opposite equivalent of creation.'
                                    The Crown

I Reductive Energy
in The Rainbow

In *The Rainbow* as in Lawrence's work at large, the vitalistic virtues—spontaneity, untamed energy, intensity of being, power—are endorsed elaborately. But the endorsement is noticeably more ambiguous on some occasions than on others. The vitality of the young Will Brangwen (he reminds Anna 'of some animal, some mysterious animal that lived in the darkness under the leaves and never came out, but which lived vividly, swift and intense') is one thing; the vitality that Will and Anna eventually release in themselves in their bouts of natural-unnatural sensuality is another. So for that matter is Ursula's fierce salt-burning corrosiveness under the moon, or the corrupt African potency of Skrebensky. In the one instance life is affirmed directly, positively, unambiguously, if also with potential ferocity and violence—but in the other instances reductively, in disintegration or corruption.

Here then, one would have thought, is a distinction of some thematic importance; yet, curiously, the final effect of the novel is to play the distinction down. The power of the horses which threaten and terrify Ursula in the last chapter is, we sense, significantly different from the corrosive menace of Ursula herself in the moonlight, and we feel that somehow the difference ought to tell in the story; yet nothing is made of it. It is of course a difference-in-similarity. In each case we are concerned with the menace of power in unmitigated assertion and it has in fact been argued, by H. M. Daleski, that Ursula's traumatic adventure recapitulates symbolically the decisive moments in her soul's journey, re-enacting her past surrenders to 'the anarchy of elemental passion'.[1] But although, positioned as it is, the episode would appear to make some

45

claim to summational significance, the claim is in fact only partially substantiated. If indeed, as Daleski has argued, the 'pressing, pressing, pressing' of the horses refers us back to the sort of assertion to which Ursula herself had resorted with Skrebensky, a frenetic assertion of her feminine self in the endeavour to burst free to fulness of being, it must still be said that there is a great deal in her relationship with her lover to which the episode, so interpreted, has no relevance. For what has this display of massive equine power to do with the explosive life-affirmation of the Ursula who most lives in our imaginations, the corrosive-disintegrative Ursula whose affirmation of life is at the same time a reduction of life? And after all it is this paradoxical Ursula who is the growing point as well as the strength of the novel in its latter phases; it is she who points forward most emphatically to *Women in Love.*

Moreover, Ursula's corrosiveness is anticipated by her father's; the one story has its roots deep in the other. So if the significance of the later story is not caught up adequately into the final chapter, the same is true, inevitably, of the earlier one. It is the *recurrent* exploration into the reductive processes that, more than anything else, gives continuity and shape to the novel; and by the same token it is the failure to realize the full cumulative significance of the discoveries made in the course of that exploration that does most to account for one's sense, towards the end, of a richness of meaning that has not altogether found its proper form. This at any rate is the case I propose to argue in the present chapter. 'The novel is the highest example of subtle inter-relatedness that man has discovered', Lawrence was to claim later.[2] It is just this inter-relatedness that we find wanting, too often, in the latter half of *The Rainbow.*

In the chapter 'Anna Victrix' we remark the partial emergence of a syndrome of images that was to prove crucial in the articulation of the reductive theme in *Women in Love*; and no passage is more prophetic than the following, with its ambiguous stress on enforced *downward* movement.

> At first she went on blithely enough with him shut down beside her. But then his spell began to take hold of her. The dark, seething potency of him, the power of a creature that lies hidden and exerts its will to the destruction of the free-running creature, as the tiger lying in the darkness of the leaves steadily enforces the fall and death of the light creatures that drink by the waterside in the morning, gradually began to take effect on her. Though he lay there

in his darkness and did not move, yet she knew he lay waiting for her. She felt his will fastening on her and pulling her down, even whilst he was silent and obscure.

She found that, in all her outgoings and her incomings, he prevented her. Gradually she realized that she was being borne down by him, borne down by the clinging, heavy weight of him, that he was pulling her down as a leopard clings to a wild cow and exhausts her and pulls her down. . . .

Why did he want to drag her down, and kill her spirit? Why did he want to deny her spirit? Why did he deny her spirituality, hold her for a body only? And was he to claim her carcase? . . . 'What do you do to me?' she cried . . . 'There is something horrible in you, something dark and beastly in your will'.

Will's reductive activity is potent, vital, sanctioned by Nature (assimilated, that is, to the splendid destructiveness of leopards and tigers) but also debilitating, *un*-natural, monstrous. The downward tug is a degradation, an obscenity: 'And was he to claim her carcase?' Whether Will is 'actually' as monstrous as he seems to Anna is not of course a critical issue. There is no way of going behind the words themselves to unverbalized facts, and what the words present us with is something like an antinomy—a vision of horror and perversity imposed, immediately, upon a no less cogent vision of potency and life. What we carry away is an impression not so much of complexity of 'character' as of the value-and-cost of living within the darkness.

And the same is true of the way Will's impressively rendered sensuality is directly overlaid by his agonizing sense of vacuity and dependence; he is extremely vulnerable, and at the same time powerful. This point needs to be laboured a little, because of the way the dependence and weakness have been dwelt upon in critical commentaries and the potency correspondingly ignored. Of the potency we are assured again and again:

> There was something thick, dark, dense, powerful about him that irritated her too deeply for her to speak of it.

or:

> And ever and again he appeared as the dread flame of power. Sometimes, when he stood in the doorway, his face lit up, he seemed like an Annunciation to her, her heart beat fast. And she watched him, suspended. He had a dark, burning being that she dreaded and resisted.

Yet Daleski permits himself to remark that Will is 'the weak, if not quite the broken, end of the arch';[3] and he concludes that the conflict between Will and Anna 'derives, ultimately, from *his* imperfections'. One wonders then how it is that Anna should come in time to sustain herself with her husband's subterranean strength:

> She learned not to dread and to hate him, but to fill herself with him, to give herself to his black, sensual power, that was hidden all the daytime.

On the other hand we are not allowed to forget that the power Will mediates in the darkness is paid for by an acquaintance with the *terrors* of the darkness—and the obscenities too.

> She wanted to desert him, to leave him a prey to the open, with the unclean dogs of the darkness setting on to devour him. He must beat her, and make her stay with him.

In the paragraph immediately preceding we find this:

> And, at the bottom of her soul, she felt he wanted her to be dark, unnatural. Sometimes, when he seemed like the darkness covering and smothering her, she revolted almost in horror, and struck at him.

Will is terrified of the unclean creatures of the dark; yet in Anna's eyes he is one of those creatures himself, potent, sinister, horrifying. In short, what at one moment is potency becomes at the next, with a sudden shift of perspective, vulnerability. Nor are terror and horror absolute qualities —or static; they create, or convert themselves into their opposites: '*Because* she dreaded him and held him in horror, he became wicked, he wanted to destroy'; 'And he began to shudder . . . He must beat her, and make her stay with him'. In both Will and Anna power is a function of vulnerability and vulnerability of power.

The reading Leavis offers then seems to me to do these scenes less than justice:

> Anna, on the face of it, might seem to be the aggressor. The relevant aspect of her has its clear dramatization in the scene that led to the banning of the book; the scene in which she is surprised by Will dancing the defiant triumph of her pregnancy, naked in her bedroom. She is the Magna Mater, the type-figure adverted to so much in *Women in Love* of a feminine dominance that must defeat the growth of any prosperous long-term relation between a man and a woman.

But we have to recognize that this dominance in Anna has for its complement a dependence in Will. There are passages that convey to us with the most disturbing force the paradoxical insufferableness to Anna of such a dependence, and its self-frustrating disastrousness. This inability to stand alone constitutes a criticism of a positive trait of Will's towards which Anna feels a deep antipathy. In a sense that Lawrence's art defines very clearly, he is religious. It is a religiousness that provokes in Anna a destructive rationalism, and the scenes that give us the clash leave us in no doubt that both attitudes are being criticized. The whole treatment of religion in this chapter, called 'Anna Victrix', which deals with it directly in a sustained way, is very subtle in its distinctions and its delicacies.

This, surely, is too rationalistic, and moralistic, to convey a full sense of the paradoxical richness of the text.* Will doesn't, or shouldn't, lose marks for his inability to stand alone. What should register with us rather is the manifest weakness-in-strength; this, we have to recognize, is what it is like to be a natural inhabitant of the darkness. In other words, it is not so much that 'attitudes are being criticized' as that we are being made aware of the cost of a certain kind of human experience. The potency and the capacity for degradation—the fear of the night and the splendid dark sensuality—belong to a single individual, and what is being deviously suggested is that the potency can't be had *without* the degradation. The more sophisticated strategy of *Women in Love* is already within sight.

If the endorsement of reductive power in 'Anna Victrix' is largely oblique, by the time we reach the chapter 'The Child' it has become explicit, though not, for that reason, unambiguous. First there is the account of Will's unconsummated seduction of the young girl he meets in Nottingham. A moralistic interpretation of this scene, entailing a simple ethical judgment on Will's perversity and pursuit of sensation for its own sake, would drastically impoverish its significance.

* It is worth remarking, moreover, that Anna, when she dances naked, is *not* the Magna Mater, or at all like the figure adverted so much in *Women in Love*, as the insistent imagery of fertility alone should warn us.[4]

> He did not care about her, except that he wanted to
> overcome her resistance, to have her in his power, fully
> and exhaustively to enjoy her.

This and similar passages, taken out of context, could be used to support the view that the whole episode points the distance between a fully human sexuality and the aridness of unassimilated desire.

> Just his own senses were supreme. All the rest was
> external, insignificant, leaving him alone with this girl
> whom he wanted to absorb, whose properties he wanted
> to absorb into his own senses. . . .
> But he was patiently working for her relaxation, patiently,
> his whole being fixed in the smile of latent gratification, his
> whole body electric with a subtle, powerful, reducing
> force upon her.

Yet this premeditated sensuality (one notes how often Lawrence resorts to the image of electricity to suggest the *frisson* of white or sensational sex) opens up for Will a new world of Absolute Beauty.

> And his hand that grasped her side felt one curve of her,
> and it seemed like a new creation to him, a reality, an
> absolute, an existing tangible beauty of the absolute.

Clearly, the human value of Will's experience is by no means easily determined. Indeed its final value *cannot* be determined; the effect of Lawrence's art is to discourage in the reader any tendency to reach a single and ready-defined judgment. The destruction of the flesh in conscious sensuality is presented very deliberately for contemplation, as though the intention were to invite a dismissive moral judgment; but, just as deliberately, any such judgment is held at bay. The perversity and destructiveness are fully conceded and, artistically, fully realized; but so is the beauty, the 'amazing beauty and pleasure'. As so often in Lawrence's work the effect is one of double exposure: we register the impulse to destruction even while we acknowledge the enhancement of life.

These complexities and tensions are sustained and indeed intensified in the sequence that follows when Will, returning home, incites Anna to a new kind of love-making, 'a sensuality violent and extreme as death'.

> There was no tenderness, no love between them any
> more, only the maddening, sensuous lust for discovery
> and the insatiable, exorbitant gratification in the sensual
> beauties of her body. . . .
> They accepted shame, and were one with it in their most

unlicensed pleasures. It was incorporated. It was a bud that blossomed into beauty and heavy, fundamental gratification.

Mark Spilka's comment on these pages, in *The Love Ethic of D. H. Lawrence*, runs as follows:

> They revel in one another, as Tom Brangwen and his wife had revelled before them, and as Rupert and Ursula (Brangwen) Birkin would revel after them, in order to root out all shame, all fear of the body's secrets: . . .
>
> Here Lawrence seems to find a place, in marriage, for cold, lustful desire (as opposed, apparently, to 'hot, living desire'); and its function—a limited one—is discovery and purification: a sensual revel, a phallic 'hunting out' which leaves one free for the deeper, warmer love he generally upholds. But more than this, the experience sets Brangwen free to attend to his public tasks, which he had hitherto endured as so much mechanical activity. Now his purposive self is roused and released, and he begins at 30 to teach woodwork classes at the Cossethay night-school. About ten years later he returns to his own creative work in wood and other materials, and soon afterwards he receives an appointment as Art and Handwork Instructor for the County of Nottingham. Through the purgation process, both he and his wife have been aroused to active, purposive life—she, from the long sleep of motherhood; he, from social sterility to a point of social and self-respect.

And in a footnote, after quoting a comparable scene from *Lady Chatterley's Lover* ('Burning out the shames, the deepest, oldest shames, in the most secret places . . .') he adds:

> What the experience does for Constance Chatterley it also does for Will and Anna Brangwen. It is a purgation process, and less the norm of love than a release to full, creative life.

This reading is faithful to the text up to a point, for Brangwen's profound sensual activity does release in him a socially purposive self. And yet what we observe first and foremost is that the new licentiousness has an absolute, or non-instrumental, value. Obviously (for the language is quite explicit) Will's sensuality is disintegrative. A deliberate, piecemeal exploitation of the body takes the place of tenderness and love. Yet this disintegrative sex is now discovered to be a way-in to life, and, above all, a revelation of beauty, 'supreme, immoral, Absolute Beauty'. This is the bold truth we are required to confront; and Spilka's reading tends to dissipate it.* It is the final paragraphs of the chapter that that reading is most relevant to, for there we find ourselves in a more reassuring, not to say cosy world, where social purposiveness is triumphant and even lust turns (eventually) a moral mill.

> He wanted to be unanimous with the whole of purposive mankind . . . For the first time he began to take real interest in a public affair. He had at length, from his profound sensual activity, developed a real purposive self.

The *rapprochement* effected between the reductive and the creative in these last paragraphs impresses one as willed and glib, indeed as largely unreal. We are not to be convinced by mere assertion that social purposiveness can develop out of sensuality and a profound moral in-

* Kinhead-Weekes, too, while acknowledging the positive virtue in Will's licentiousness, seems to me to partly take back what he concedes, and to slyly introduce irrelevant moralistic criteria. 'Of course', he remarks, we are not 'meant to see' the way of pure darkness, or lust, as 'an equal alternative' to the way of love and creativity.

> (Will and Anna) become discoverers, and what they discover is 'Absolute Beauty'.
> This new relationship is, however, sharply distinguished from their relation as lovers. It exists entirely in terms of lust. . . . They 'die' and are renewed, but it is 'pure death', purely dark, and a renewal of the dark side of themselves only. A great part of their total personalities has to be excluded. (*ibid*, pp. 391–3)

There is insufficient recognition here of the fact that Will's lust is only one aspect of that multiform energy of disintegration which counts so much in the life of *The Rainbow* from the chapter 'Anna Victrix' on (though Kinhead Weekes does note the affinity between Will's lust and the African corruption of Skrebensky). Significant, in this connection, is the remark that the new relationship is 'sharply distinguished' from the relationship which has obtained between the lovers previously. For in fact, if the two kinds of relationship are distinguished sharply at one level, at another level they certainly are not; as I suggested above, Will's licentiousness belongs, recognizably enough, with his impulse to drag Anna *down* into the darkness: both kinds of activity are unnatural, perverse, reductive. Like Spilka, Kinhead-Weekes is prevented from acknowledging the centrality and pervasiveness of reductive energy in Lawrence's fiction, and its characteristically positive-negative value, by preconceptions that are partly moralistic, partly organicist; he cannot admit the distintegrative impulse to be an 'equal alternative' to the integrative. On the evidence of Lawrence's art, however, as we have it before us in *The Rainbow*, this, I submit, is precisely the admission that the reader *must* make.

difference; this, surely, is comething that calls for patient demonstration.

On the other hand the 'mere assertion' was in itself an achievement; Lawrence was breaking new ground, even if he was doing so at a purely discursive level. To gauge the distance, as it were, between the 'argument' of the paragraphs under review and the 'argument' of the paragraphs that conclude the preceding chapter, 'The Cathedral', is one way of enforcing this point.

> He still remained motionless, seething with inchoate rage, when his whole nature seemed to disintegrate. He seemed to live with a strain upon himself, and occasionally came these dark, chaotic rages, the lust for destruction. She then fought with him, and their fights were horrible, murderous. And then the passion between them came just as black and awful. . . .
>
> He made himself a woodwork shed, in which to restore things which were destroyed in the church. So he had plenty to do: his wife, his child, the church, the woodwork, and his wage-earning, all occupying him. If only there were not some limit to him, some darkness across his eyes! . . . He was unready for fulfilment. Something undeveloped in him, there was a darkness in him which he *could* not unfold, which would never unfold in him.

This might well seem to be more honest than the conclusion to the chapter that follows; for Will's lust for destruction, of which we have heard so much and which we now recognize as a basic fact about him, is not lost sight of at all, even while we are being assured of his constructiveness and purposiveness. In other words, the creative and the reductive co-exist throughout; the one is not simply *substituted* for the other, as in the later passage, which seems by comparison a good deal too smooth. On the other hand the theme of the later passage is intrinsically more 'difficult'. Whereas in the earlier instance Will's creativeness and destructiveness, if undissociated are also causally unconnected, in the later instance it is actually *from* the destructiveness (in this case disintegrative sensuality) that the creativeness, we are to believe, proceeds, or develops. In cold fact however, the total failure to dramatize this development means that the destructive and the creative seem no more inwardly affiliated than they were in the earlier sequence. Indeed less so; virtually they lose contact.

And it is a loss of contact of just this kind that we frequently remark in the remaining chapters. The story repeatedly concerns itself with disintegration and destructiveness; and we can scarcely fail to assume, as we proceed, that it will be part of this concern to discover and define a significant pattern of relationships between *kinds* of disintegration: *this* disintegrative process will prove to have a bearing on *that*. But in the event no such pattern emerges; 'cross-reference' seems both to be encouraged and not encouraged. There is the fiercely corrosive and violently destructive activity of Ursula in the moonlight; there is the corruption and social disintegration at Wiggiston, and the corresponding despair of Ursula herself—('She had no connexion with other people. Her lot was isolated and deadly. There was nothing for her anywhere, but this black disintegration'); there is the splendid-sinister potency of Skrebensky, corrupt, fecund, destructive ('He kissed her, and she quivered as if she were being destroyed, shattered'); and there is Ursula's vision of advancing corruption at the very end of the novel. But to what extent these kinds of disintegration bear upon each other is not clear. Whereas in *Women in Love* the densely reticulated imagery is constantly persuading us to see identities in difference, to make discriminations and discover analogies, in the latter part of *The Rainbow* we seem to be invited teasingly to embark on this same procedure only in the end to be frustrated.

But these judgments require substantiating and I turn first to the scene, in the chapter 'First Love', in which the adolescent Ursula annihilates her lover under the moon. Once again (as in the case of Will Brangwen, 'the sensual male seeking his pleasure') we find ourselves acknowledging a value in activity patently opposed to the creative and integrative. 'But hard and fierce she had fastened upon him, cold as the moon and burning as a fierce salt . . . seething like some cruel, corrosive salt'. 'Cold . . . and burning': the oxymoron (a common one wherever Lawrence is concerned with the reductive processes) focusses the sense of an inverse vitality running counter to growth and to warm organic blood desire. Nowhere in the novel is human personality reduced more obviously and more drastically to the inhuman and inorganic, and yet nowhere are we more aware of power and energy humanly mediated. The recurrent images—moonlight, steel, corrosive salt, the sea—exclude the organic entirely, and one thinks of the famous letter on Marinetti and the Futurists (5 June, 1914):

> . . . it is the inhuman will, call it physiology, or like Marinetti—physiology of matter, that fascinates me. I don't so much care about what the woman *feels*—in the ordinary usage of the word. That presumes an *ego* to feel with. . . . You mustn't look in my novel for the old stable *ego* of the character.

In a stimulating article on *The Narrative Technique of "The Rainbow"*.[5] Roger Sale has considered the literary means by which Lawrence contrived to 'break down "the old stable ego of character"'. It is not so much Sale's argument itself that concerns me here as the significance of that metaphor of 'breaking down'.

> The simplest declarative sentence is one of the main aids the novelist has in building up a stable ego, an identity. . . .
>
> If we turn to a passage in *The Rainbow*, we can show how Lawrence tries there to break down this natural building-up process . . .

The phrasing could not be more apt—or revealing; for 'breaking down' is a common Laurentian synonym for 'reduction'. So Sale pays his tribute unconsciously to the iconic power of Lawrence's art, and demonstrates indirectly that the major novels are about the reductive process not only in the most obvious or literal sense but in the further sense that they themselves image that process. In the episode under review we remark how the fiercely corrosive activity of the fictive Ursula is matched, and to that extent endorsed, by the corrosive activity—no less vigorous—of the artist himself. And this endorsement goes far towards explaining why our moral sense should fail to be outraged by Ursula's 'enormous wilfulness'.[6] Her attitude to Skrebensky is inhuman, but then so is the novelist's art, in the sense that part of what he is engaged in is the reduction of human personality to an inhuman or material substratum. But this involves no diminishing of artistic intensity; indeed it has the reverse effect, and the novelist creates a notable artificial beauty—a beauty 'immoral and against mankind'.[7]

Probably the best gloss on these pages is a passage that I have already quoted from *The Crown*. (It is a passage significant also for the kind of bearing it does *not* have on the episode or on the novel generally, as I shall argue later.)

> Leonardo knew this: he knew the strange endlessness of the flux of corruption. It is Mona Lisa's ironic smile. Even Michael Angelo knew it. It is in his *Leda and the Swan*. For the swan is one of the symbols of divine corruption with its reptile feet buried in the ooze and mud, its voluptuous form yielding and embracing the ooze of water, its beauty white and cold and terrifying, like the dead beauty of the moon, like the water-lily, the sacred lotus, its neck and head like the snake, it is for us a flame of the cold white fire of flux, the phosphorescence of corruption, the salt,

cold burning of the sea which corrodes all it touches, coldly reduces every sun-built form to ash, to the original elements. This is the beauty of the swan, the lotus, the snake, this cold white salty fire of infinite reduction. And there was some suggestion of this in the Christ of the early Christians, the Christ who was the Fish.

The paradoxes are a good deal sharper in the novel than in the essay (with the exception of that last equation of Christ and Fish), for the obvious reason that Ursula, a human being, is further removed than snake or swan from 'the original elements', so that in the novel the reductive process is that much more spectacular. For all that, we are not more interested in the morality of Ursula's behaviour, essentially, than we would be in the behaviour of swan or snake. Or, to make the point perhaps less provocatively, we are interested in the morality of her behaviour only to the extent that we are interested in her dehumanization. It is relevant to recall that remarkable passage in E.T.'s Memoir where an account is given of three occasions on which Lawrence became wildly distraught—possessed—under the combined influence of moonlight and sea:

> I was really frightened then—not physically, but deep in my soul. He created an atmosphere not of death which after all is part of mortality, but of an utter negation of life, as though he had become dehumanized.[8]

Analogously, in the scene in *The Rainbow*, one is impressed not so much by Ursula's will to separateness, or her frenetic feminine assertiveness, though these qualities are doubtless evident enough, as by her intimidating inhuman-ness.* Yet the further she departs from the warmly living the more evidence she gives of vitality of a different kind—inverse, disintegrative. Inverse is Birkin's word; and indeed his notion of 'inverse process' is loosely relevant to the whole episode.

> When the stream of synthetic creation lapses, we find ourselves part of the inverse process, the blood of destructive creation. Aphrodite is born in the first spasm of universal dissolution—then the snakes and swans and lotus—

* The de-humanizing process is associated with the salt sea in the Melville essay too:

> Away, away from humanity. To the sea. The naked salt, elemental sea. To go to sea, to escape humanity.
> The human heart gets into a frenzy at last, in its desire to dehumanize itself.   (*final version*).

marsh-flowers—and Gudrun and Gerald—born in the
process of destructive creation . . . It is a progressive
process—and it ends in universal nothing . . .

The process can end only in a re-assimilation to the anonymous energies
of nature; yet it is productive of a deadly and distinctive beauty. And
in *The Rainbow*, likewise, beauty is a product of the reductive process, a
function of reductive power.

She stood for some moments out in the overwhelming
luminosity of the moon. She seemed a beam of gleaming
power. She was afraid of what she was. Looking at him,
at his shadowy, unreal, wavering presence a sudden lust
seized her, to lay hold of him and tear him and make him
into nothing. Her hands and wrists felt immeasurably hard
and strong, like blades.

This revelation of life and beauty where we might scarcely be supposed
to expect it, in a process that brutally affronts our sympathies—in a
progressive departure from the human—is what the episode is centrally
about. (It is for the most part a fully realized rhetorical beauty and
rhetorical life, though there is, surely, some overwriting.) To identify
with Ursula's daytime consciousness, and accept as self-validating the
slow horror she experiences as she gradually recovers herself (as one
critic has done)[9] is clearly inappropriate. Primarily, Ursula's horror is
there to measure the recession of the magical and mythic. There is no
suggestion that the familiar order of reality is the more valid or true; it is
simply different.

And indeed the sheer fact of difference is stated as cogently as could
well be. It is a question however whether the statement is not in fact too
cogent. I have suggested, apropos of the final paragraphs of the chapter
'The Child', that Lawrence's task is to communicate a sense of the
distinction between pure creation and destructive creation—or the vital
and the perversely vital—without effecting a simple dissociation between
them. In the earlier sequences involving Tom and Lydia, and Anna and
Will, the constant modulation from the mythic to the commonplace, and
vice versa, has established the existence of a consciousness at once
distinct from our familiar daytime consciousness and at the same time
prone to assert itself in the context of daytime living. Will's murderously
reductive activity in the chapter 'Anna Victrix' is a quality of his everyday behaviour and also the utterance of a self that can seem at moments
extravagantly alien. But from the stackyard scene on there is a tendency

for the magical and the everyday—the subterranean self and the social self—to move apart. And the abrupt dissociation of personae at the end of the scene, when Ursula repudiates her 'corrosive self' with horror (while the night is suddenly 'struck back into its old, accustomed, mild reality') is, in this connection, only too suggestive of what is to come. A truth is enforced, but at the expense of a counter-truth; Ursula's ruthless energy is made to seem *merely* alien.

It is Skrebensky's character however that tends most conspicuously to bifurcate, and in a way that bears even more suggestively on my argument. If it is a mistake to interpret Ursula's lurid behaviour under the moon with a moralistic bias, it is a parallel mistake to ignore the corrupt vitality of her lover and to write him off as a hollow man *simpliciter*. Leavis has perhaps led the way here; at any rate he has concerned himself exclusively with Skrebensky's shortcomings, laying stress upon his 'good-citizen acceptance of the social function as the ultimate meaning of life' and pointing to the connection between this acceptance and his 'inadequacy as a lover'. Others, designedly or not, have followed suit. S. L. Goldberg lumps Skrebensky with Winifred Inger and Tom Brangwen, 'the irrevocably lost'.[10] Daleski, quoting the argument between Ursula and Skrebensky about being a soldier, comments:

> This passage establishes not only that Skrebensky is 'not exactly' a soldier, but that he is not exactly anything. If, unlike Will, he does not deny the outside world, he accepts his place in it with a mechanical and unadventurous complacency. . . .
> Skrebensky is even less defined as a man than either Tom or Will; lacking the rooted stability of the one and the passionate aspiration of the other, he has no real identity.[11]

But what of the Skrebensky who, like Ursula herself, can be a vehicle of intense vitality, positive-reductive, potent, corrupt?

> He talked to her all the while in low tones about Africa, conveying something strange and sensual to her: the negro, with his loose, soft passion that could envelop one like a bath. Gradually he transferred to her the hot, fecund darkness that possessed his own blood. He was strangely secret. The whole world must be abolished. . . .

> He seemed like the living darkness upon her, she was
> in the embrace of the strong darkness. He held her
> enclosed, soft, unutterably soft, and with the unrelaxing
> softness of fate, the relentless softness of fecundity. . . .
> It was bliss, it was the nucleolating of the fecund dark-
> ness. Once the vessel had vibrated till it was shattered,
> the light of consciousness gone, then the darkness reigned,
> and the unutterable satisfaction.

Here again is that effect of double exposure to which I have already alluded: on the one hand an impression of cultural and organic regression, on the other hand the sensual transfiguration, 'the unutterable satis-faction'. It is the familiar paradox:

> 'Corruption will at last break down for us the deadened
> forms, and release us into the infinity.'

The image of the turgid African night is parallel to those other images of potency-in-disintegration, the flaring moon and the salt-burning sea. Skrebensky's sensuality is at once reductive, regressive, a breaking down ('One breathes it, like a smell of blood', 'The whole world must be abolished') and a release into infinity. The sensual ecstasy has its roots in corruption. The lovers inhabit an 'unblemished darkness'; yet the matrix (as it were) of this darkness is that other, sinister darkness of Africa. This latter is the darkness that sustains them, ultimately—as the swan has its reptile feet buried in the ooze and mud. We are in the world of *Women in Love*. The teeming night is recognizably Birkin's 'dark river of dissolution': 'massive and *fluid* with terror', 'his loose, soft passion that could envelop one like a *bath*', 'they walked the darkness beside the massive *river*', 'the soft *flow* of his kiss . . . the warm fecund flow of his kiss', 'one fecund nucleus of the *fluid* darkness'. This is very obviously in the spirit of the later novel. It anticipates Birkin's '*fountain* of mystic corruption'.

Yet the Ursula-Skrebensky story, it is commonly agreed, is not, by a long way, as coherent or compelling as for the most part the story of *Women in Love* is. And one reason at least is plain. The final move-ment of *The Rainbow* is organized around a single human relationship. Inevitably this deprives Lawrence of the scope he needed for elaborating those paradoxical themes which, all the evidence goes to show, were now so deeply engaging his imagination. It is no accident that the single pair of lovers became two pairs of lovers in the sequel; they had to. Skrebensky is called on to discharge the functions of both Birkin *and* Gerald, to 'figure', in Jamesian phrase, the possibilities both for life *and* death in reductive sexuality. Not surprisingly he proves unequal to the task. At a non-narrative level the paradox about living disintegration can be developed and protracted as far as ingenuity will allow; but at the narrative level the limits to this process are stricter. *The Rainbow* is a novel, with a story. Skrebensky cannot, in the story, be given over finally to disintegration and also be redeemed. And, in the event, under these novelistic pressures his character falls apart into *two* characters.

On the one hand there is Skrebensky the darkly potent lover, inhabitant of the fecund universal night.

> Everything he did was a voluptuous pleasure to him—
> either to ride on horseback, or to walk, or to lie in the sun,
> or to drink in a public-house. He had no use for people,
> nor for words. He had an amused pleasure in everything, a
> great sense of voluptuous richness in himself . . .

There is little doubt that we are to accept this vitality as real. Moreover it entails a certain correlative distinction at a more personal and conscious level.

> She took him home, and he stayed a week-end at
> Beldover with her family. She loved having him in the
> house. Strange how he seemed to come into the atmosphere
> of her family, with his laughing, insidious grace. They all
> loved him, he was kin to them. His raillery, his warm,
> voluptuous mocking presence was meat and joy to the
> Brangwen household. For this house was always quivering
> with darkness, they put off their puppet form when they
> came home, to lie and drowse in the sun.

The emphasis here is still on the dark under-life; yet laughing insidious grace, raillery, warmth and voluptuous mockery also suggest less esoteric qualities—more 'human' and social—and a corresponding fulness or completeness of being. At any rate we are left in no doubt of the richness and abundance of life which the relationship with Skrebensky, for all its limitations, does release. The lovers are held together *only* in the sensual subconsciousness, yet that only includes so much.

> Then he turned and kissed her, and she waited for him.
> The pain to her was the pain she wanted, the agony was the
> agony she wanted. She was caught up, entangled in the
> powerful vibration of the night. The man, what was he ?—
> a dark, powerful vibration that encompassed her. She
> passed away as on a dark wind, far, far away, into the

pristine darkness of paradise, into the original immortality.
She entered the dark fields of immortality.

In the face of this and similar passages it is scarcely adequate to say of
Skrebensky that though he satisfies Ursula 'time after time in their
physical relations' he fails her at the last in the "beyondness of sex" . . .
—where Birkin in *Women in Love* will not fail with Ursula later'.[12]
Something like this, it is true, is Ursula's own reading of the situation:

> The salt, bitter passion of the sea, its indifference to the
> earth, its swinging definite motion, its strength, its attack,
> and its salt burning, seemed to provoke her to a pitch of
> madness, tantalizing her with vast suggestions of fulfilment.
> And then, for personification, would come Skrebensky,
> Skrebensky, whom she knew, whom she was fond of, who
> was attractive, but whose soul could not contain her in its
> waves of strength, nor his breast compel her in burning,
> salty passion:

But we remember not only how she and Skrebensky had 'stood together,
dark, fluid, *infinitely* potent, giving the living lie to the dead whole which
contained them' or had passed away 'into the pristine darkness of
paradise', or how 'perfectly and supremely free' they were, 'proud
beyond all question, and *surpassing mortal conditions*', but also the sinister
African potency, the destructiveness and indifference to humanity which
Skrebensky had darkly communicated and which, I have argued, are
analogous to the 'salt, bitter passion' which, we now learn, he is utterly
deficient in.

But then of course there is the other Skrebensky.

> His life lay in the established order of things. He had his
> five senses too. They were to be gratified. . . .
>   The good of the greatest number was all that mattered.
> That which was the greatest good for them all, collectively,
> was the greatest good for the individual.

This is the Skrebensky the commentators have fixed upon—a vacuity;
a mere social integer, essentially without identity and living in pure
externality through the senses.

It is true that the contrast between the two Skrebenskys is not
always as steep as the passages quoted might suggest. There are moments
when the vacuity and the power live together convincingly, are accepted
as belonging to a single person.

> He seemed so balanced and sure, he made such a confident presence. He was a great rider, so there was about him some of a horseman's sureness, and habitual definiteness of decision, also some of the horseman's animal darkness. Yet his soul was only the more wavering, vague . . . She could only feel the dark, heavy fixity of his animal desire. . . . all must be kept so dark, the consciousness must admit nothing . . . He was always side-tracking, always side-tracking his own soul. She could see him so well out there, in India—one of the governing class, superimposed upon an old civilisation, lord and master of a clumsier civilisation than his own.

Here Skrebensky's limitations are a believable aspect of his strength; the animal darkness, the fixity of animal desire, the disinclination to bring things to consciousness, the side-tracking of his own soul—this all hangs together. If his soul is wavering and vague, if he virtually has no soul, this is not because he lives purely in the senses, but because he has the inarticulateness of an animal—both its dark power and its heavy fixity.

And if Skrebensky's sensual being impresses us as far shallower on some occasions than on others, something similar is true of Ursula. She however is always exempted from adverse judgment.

> Yet she loved him, the body of him, whatever his decisions might be . . . She caught his brilliant, burnished glamour. Her heart and her soul were shut away fast down below, hidden. She was free of them. She was to have her satisfaction.

We may compare this with the earlier comment on Skrebensky: 'He had his five senses too. They were to be gratified'. But whereas in the one instance dissociated sensuality releases a glow and splendour of life ('She became proud and erect, like a flower, putting itself forth in its proper strength') in the other it is a token of death ('Skrebensky, somehow, had created a deadness around her, a sterility, as if the world were ashes . . . Why did he never really want a woman, not with the whole of him: never love, never worship, only just physically want her ?') When Skrebensky finally fails Ursula at the end, they are engaged in a pursuit of just that kind of satisfaction which she herself had set up as a goal ('Her heart and soul were shut away . . . She was to have her satisfaction'); yet responsibility for this failure seems to be laid exclusively at Skrebensky's door.

> She liked it, the electric fire of the silk under his hands upon
> her limbs . . . Yet she did not feel beautiful. All the time,
> she felt she was not beautiful to him, only exciting. She
> let him take her, and he seemed mad, mad with excited
> passion. But she, as she lay afterwards on the cold, soft
> sand, looking up at the blotted, faintly luminous sky, felt
> that she was as cold now as she had been before.

The transfiguration in the flesh which Ursula had unquestionably en-
joyed with Skrebensky is here repudiated, and the intoxication of the
senses which they shared is conceived of as having ended in itself; it
involved, apparently, 'no connexion with the unknown'. But the
reader's recollections, as I have suggested, are different from Ursula's,
and are not so rapidly erased.

One can conceive easily enough of an ending to the novel which
would seem to resolve these warring tensions: Ursula, looking back in
gratitude to the very real satisfaction and fulfilment Skrebensky had
brought, might yet acknowledge that in the end the sensual ecstasy could
not in itself sustain her. Yet, clearly, tensions as powerful as these are not
to be resolved so neatly and rationally. For Lawrence is under an evident
compulsion to make *incompatible* statements about voluptuousness or
dissociated sensuality, and is struggling to find a novelistic pattern
sufficiently flexible to allow him to do so. The pattern to which he is
committed is transparently *not* sufficiently flexible; so we find him
asserting of Skrebensky that his sensuality ends in sensuality and yet
also that it leads into the unknown.

There is an essay of this period, *The Lemon Gardens* (it appeared in
the *English Review* in September 1913) in which this doubleness of
attitude to self-conscious sensuality is articulated with especial clarity.

> This is the soul of the Italian since the Renaissance. In
> the sunshine he basks asleep, gathering up a vintage into
> his veins which in the night-time he will distil into ecstatic
> sensual delight, the intense, white-cold ecstasy of darkness
> and moonlight, the raucous, cat-like, destructive enjoy-
> ment, the senses conscious and crying out in their con-
> sciousness in the pangs of the enjoyment, which has con-
> sumed the southern nation, perhaps all the Latin races,
> since the Renaissance. . . .
> This is one way of transfiguration into the eternal
> flame, the transfiguration through ecstasy in the flesh. . . .
> And this is why the Italian is attractive, supple, and
> beautiful, because he worships the Godhead in the flesh.

63

> We envy him, we feel pale and insignificant beside him. Yet at the same time we feel superior to him, as if he were a child and we adult.
>
> Wherein are we superior? Only because we went beyond the phallus in the search of the Godhead, the creative origin. And we found the physical forces and the secrets of science. . . .
>
> But we have exhausted ourselves in the process. We have found great treasures, and we are now impotent to use them. So we have said: 'What good are these treasures, they are vulgar nothings.' We have said: 'Let us go back from this adventuring, let us enjoy our own flesh, like the Italian.' But our habit of life, our very constitution, prevents our being quite like the Italian. The phallus will never serve us as a Godhead, because we do not believe in it: no Northern race does. Therefore, either we set ourselves to serve our children, calling them 'the future', or else we turn perverse and destructive, give ourselves joy in the destruction of the flesh.

'Perverse and destructive': the tone is distinctly unsympathetic. 'This is one way of transfiguration into the eternal flame': the tone is far from unsympathetic. Yet the topic is essentially the same on each occasion. True, the Italian's worship of the Godhead in the flesh is genuine, whereas the northerner's is derivative and mechanical. Yet the theme in each instance is the self-consciousness of the flesh, destructive enjoyment, the pursuit of maximum sensation, the senses conscious and crying out in their consciousness. And these in effect are the ambiguities of the Ursula-Skrebensky story. We may compare:

> She vibrated like a jet of electric, firm fluid in response. Yet she did not feel beautiful. All the time, she felt she was not beautiful to him, only exciting.

And

> But the fire is cold, as in the eyes of a cat, it is a green fire. It is fluid, electric.

In the essay the cold fire has a splendour absent from the episode in the novel.

> This is the supremacy of the flesh, which devours all, and becomes transfigured into a magnificent brindled flame, a burning bush indeed.

But as I have suggested, a dismissive note—corresponding to the 'not beautiful . . . only exciting' of the novel—is there in the essay too, in the unsympathetic attitude to the northerner's merely mechanical sensation-hunting.

And so it is that the character of Skrebensky fails in the last analysis to cohere. He is made a butt, like the northerner, because he seeks the destruction of the flesh, or pure gratification through the senses; yet just the capacity to live through the flesh, reductively, like the Italian, is his strength. It is only with *Women in Love* that Lawrence finds for this teasing paradox an appropriate dramatic correlative.

In the passage from *The Crown* which I have chosen as epigraph to the second part of this book Lawrence lists various alternative modes of the activity of departure. These are decay, corruption, destruction, and breaking down; and elsewhere in the essay he supplies others—resolving down, reduction, corrosion, decomposition, dissolution, disintegration. In *Women in Love* these various processes—in all their ambiguity as opposite equivalents of creation—are represented comprehensively; but in *The Rainbow* much less so. Decay and corruption, crucial images in the later novel, play a minor and for the most part unobtrusive role in the earlier one; moreover their value or force is not on the whole ambiguous.* In the passage in which they are most obviously deployed—the account of Ursula's visit to Wiggiston with Winifred Inger—their significance is all on the surface and noticeably uncomplicated. The marsh, in *Women in Love* foul and deadly yet also a source of perverse but genuine vitality, is here merely foul and deadly. Or very nearly so.

> Her Uncle Tom too had something marshy about him—
> the succulent moistness and turgidity, and the same
> brackish, nauseating effect of a marsh, where life and decay-
> ing are one.

The nausea is absolute and uncomplicated, it would seem; yet even here there is a hint of the ambivalence to come.

> She too, Winifred, worshipped the impure abstraction,
> the mechanisms of matter. There, there, in the machine, in
> service of the machine, was she free from the clog and
> degradation of human feeling.

The notion that to be human is necessarily to be nourished in *corruption*

---

* I do not wish to suggest that there is an absolute and necessary virtue in ambiguity. It is true that my argument in this book seems to entail that proposition, but largely because I am concerned with one aspect only of Lawrence's art.

('clog and degradation') is well within sight here, so that a cross-reference to the dominant contextual image of the marsh at any rate *begins* to be set in motion: we seem to catch at some such implied significance as that the marsh, admittedly clogging and vile, is for all that, or rather all the more for that, a source of life. The resonance is faint and apparently accidental, but prophetic of *Women in Love*, without question.

In the handling of this theme of corruption in *The Rainbow* one is indeed haunted by a sense of half-realized significance. There is the treatment of Ursula's uncle Tom for instance. Before the meeting at Wiggiston he had already made a decisive impact upon her imagination, when she saw him at the farm after the drowning of his father.

> She could see him, in all his elegant demeanour, bestial, almost corrupt. And she was frightened. She never forgot to look for the bestial, frightening side of him, after this.
> He said 'Good-bye' to his mother and went away at once. Ursula almost shrank from his kiss, now. She wanted it nevertheless, and the little revulsion as well.

And we remember this when he appears next, at the wedding (the passage is too long to quote in full).

> A kind of flame of physical desire was gradually beating up in the Marsh. . . . Tom Brangwen, with all his secret power, seemed to fan the flame that was rising. . . .
> The music began, and the bonds began to slip. Tom Brangwen was dancing with the bride, quick and fluid and as if in another element, inaccessible as the creatures that move in the water. . . . One couple after another was washed and absorbed into the deep underwater of the dance.
> 'Come', said Ursula to Skrebensky, laying her hand on his arm. . . .
> It was his will and her will locked in a trance of motion, two wills locked in one motion, yet never fusing, never yielding one to the other. It was a glaucous, intertwining, delicious flux and contest in flux.

The dichotomies of the moralist are hopelessly irrelevant here. The underworld over which the half-sinister Tom Brangwen presides is a place of dangerous licence, of enchantment, of heightened life, a place for the privileged to enter. Yet if here, in his equivocal way, Tom releases life, and later, at Wiggiston, is an unequivocal agent of death, nothing is made of this duality; it generates no significance. There is no ironic juxtaposition of his two roles, as there would be in *Women in Love*; we are not manoeuvred into adopting, simultaneously or nearly so, conflicting attitudes to corruption or decay.

The final paragraphs of the novel, which are commonly acknowledged to be unconvincing, bear upon my argument with especial force. There is a demonstrable confusion of imagery in these paragraphs, amounting in fact to a sort of trickery—but of a kind that shows Lawrence feeling his way towards the richer effects of *Women in Love*.

> She knew that the sordid people who crept hardscaled and separate on the face of the world's corruption were living still.... She saw in the rainbow the earth's new architecture, the old, brittle corruption of houses and factories swept away, the world built up in a living fabric of Truth, fitting to the over-arching heaven.

The hardness that Ursula discovers around her is both the hardness of death and a hardness that conceals new life. We are asked to believe that the one kind of hardness can become or virtually *is* the other, and on grounds that appear to be little more than verbal. 'The terrible corruption spreading over the face of the land' is *hard, dry, brittle*; and equally hard, dry and brittle is the 'horny covering of disintegration', 'the husk of an old fruition' in which Ursula can observe 'the swelling and the heaving contour of the new germination'. Lawrence insists on the completeness and seeming finality of the corruption—it is 'triumphant and unopposed'—and yet it is in the very extremity of the corruption that consolation is discovered. If organisms have everywhere disintegrated almost to dust, so much the better. The more dust-like, the more easily 'swept away'! Some such spurious logic would seem to be implied, surely, in the collocation of 'swept away', 'brittle corruption' and 'disintegration', and even if this were not so, one's other objection would remain: the hardness of corruption ('corruption so pure that it is hard and brittle') cannot be translated by mere verbal sleight-of-hand into the hardness of the husk that encloses new life.

In any case, we are left with the impression that corruption is merely *antithetical* to this new life—an impression that quite fails to correspond with the fact that the novel has been moving towards the discovery that corruption can also energize and renew. The sequence in which this movement is most emphatic is that concerned with Skrebensky's sinister African sensuality, where, as we have seen, the language affirms both the menace of corruption and its life-giving potency. (The concept of corruption is not invoked explicitly in the passage, but it is clearly within call; the African night is at once hot and fluid, and there is a powerful suggestion of over-abundant growth.) In the novel as a whole however, the movement in question, the tendency towards a simultaneous affirmation of corruption and vitality, is at least as much promise as realization.

> Awful and threatening it was, dangerous to a degree, even whilst he gave himself to it. It was pure darkness, also. All the shameful things of the body revealed themselves to him now with a sort of sinister, tropical beauty. All the shameful natural and unnatural acts of sensual voluptuousness which he and the woman partook of together, created together, they had their heavy beauty and their delight. Shame, what was it? It was part of extreme delight. It was that part of delight of which man is usually afraid. Why afraid? The secret, shameful things are most terribly beautiful.

There is not much horror in these tropics, obviously. 'Sort of' necessarily deprives 'sinister' of some of its force, and the analogy in any case is only a glancing one (by contrast one thinks of the African sequence, later, and of that very real Negro 'with his loose, soft passion'). In short, while the beauty and the energizing power of corruption (or something like corruption) are made sufficiently real, the alternative possibilities of ugliness and nausea tend to be distanced. And though this is a strategy that might appear to be locally justified, in the larger perspective it begins to look suspect. For it is in keeping with the too-easy translation of the reductive impulses into the constructive which I have already commented on apropos of the conclusion of this episode, and to that extent contributes significantly to the relative disorganization of the novel in its latter phases.

And in this respect even the African sequence suffers, excellent as it is in itself; it too is more or less dissociated. For instance, no attempt is made to relate Skrebensky's African corruption to the no less lurid corruption at Wiggiston; and yet at one level, with his belief in the priority of social values and the unimportance of the individual, Skrebensky is heading straight for that 'disintegrated lifelessness of soul' which Uncle Tom (the Wiggiston colliery-owner) and Winifred Inger, Ursula's teacher, so patently embody.

> She saw gross, ugly movements in her mistress, she saw a clayey, inert, unquickened flesh, that reminded her of the great prehistoric lizards. One day her Uncle Tom came in out of the broiling sunshine heated from walking. Then the perspiration stood out upon his head and brow, his hand was wet and hot and suffocating in its clasp. He

too had something marshy about him—the succulent
moistness and turgidity, and the same brackish, nauseating
effect of a marsh, where life and decaying are one.

'Prehistoric', 'marshy', turgidity': it is very like the African jungle. Yet
there is no particular reason why we should recall this passage, when
Skrebensky's splendid-corruptive African potency is later established.

Nor does the disintegration at Wiggiston bear as suggestively as it
might upon Ursula's disintegrative or destructive attitude to that disintegration. Nor for that matter is her destructive social attitude sharply
enough related to the destructive violence she directs against Skrebensky.
S. L. Goldberg makes a comment that is relevant here.[13]

> Of course [Lawrence] criticises [Ursula's] mistakes, her
> *affaires* with inadequate values, her immature, inarticulate
> thrashings about. On the other hand, however, her under-
> lying attitudes, her 'good heart' as it were, escape criticism
> altogether. Her characteristic Luddite reaction to in-
> dustrialism, for instance, ranges from impotent fury to
> tearful sentiment, but it is never critically placed; nor is
> the equally sentimental violence that catches, in the
> surrounding darkness, at the gleam of savage animal eyes,
> of flashing swords of overpowering 'angels', like fangs, 'not
> to be denied'. The wholesale destructiveness she un-
> leashes on Skrebensky is just this radical, apocalyptic
> mood in action. And what is remarkable is not her
> adolescence, but Lawrence's readiness to identify himself
> with her.

This is only partly acceptable; for the destructiveness Ursula unleashes
on Skrebensky has a far more ambiguous value than the pure 'apocalyptic' destructiveness implicit in her attitude to society. So it cannot just
be said that the one *is* the other. However, a valid point remains: there is
certainly an identity in the difference. Yet not enough is done to help us
to an awareness either of the difference or of the identity: Lawrence's
grasp on the relationship is not a fully inward one.

These are the kinds of dissociation then that characterize the latter
part of the novel. For all that, Lawrence is travelling perceptibly in these
pages towards the tauter organization of *Women in Love*, a work in which
the notion that 'life and decaying are one'[14] is a shaping presence throughout.

II Women in Love: *The Rhetoric of Corruption*

It is clear not only from the final pages of *The Rainbow* but also from the tenor of the argument in *The Crown*, which is work of much the same date, that the metaphor of young life stirring under an old husk, to be revealed suddenly at the due time, was likely by itself to do much less than justice to the complexity of Lawrence's evolving conceptions; for *The Crown* does not make that absolute distinction between creation and corruption which the image of the husk cannot but imply. What is most in question rather is the distinction between corruption that is creative and corruption that is not.

> When the swan first rose out of the marshes, it was a glory of creation. But when we turn back, to seek its consummation again, it is a fearful flower of corruption.
>
> And corruption, like growth, is only divine when it is pure, when all is given up to it. If it be experienced as a controlled activity within an intact whole, this is vile. When corruption goes on within the living womb, this is unthinkable.

From now on this kind of rhetoric is habitual with Lawrence. He does not cease to oppose growth sharply to decay or destruction; but this antithetical pattern is apt now to be overlaid by, or to overlay, more complicated patterns—as in the first version of the essay on Poe, already mentioned, where the death-process is registered with such rhetorical vitality, and there is such evident joy in acknowledging the harshness and violence of Necessity.

> Poe shows us the first vivid seething reduction of the
> psyche . . . It is like a tree whose fruits are perfected,
> writhing now in the grip of the first frost . . . This is how
> man must bury his own dead self: in pang after pang of
> vital, explosive self-reduction, back to the elements.

The non-organic reductive process propels us towards organic death,
and is therefore an agent of organic life. But also it is vital in its own
right, expressive of a different *kind* of life from the organic—not, like
organic life, ancient and innocent, but appropriate to our fallen state:
violent, mechanized, explosive. And the fall is at once deplored and
exulted in.

In *Women in Love* a comparable kind of doubleness is to be observed
shaping and complicating the rhetorical strategy again and again. It is
never safe to assume (as critics habitually do assume) that what is being
said about destructiveness and corruption on the surface is *all* that is
being said; almost certainly, beneath the surface, significant qualifications
are being made. There is for instance that superbly evocative account of
Beldover in the chapter 'Coal-Dust'. On the one hand the familiar
distinction of the living and the mechanical would seem to encourage
a very simple attitude of rejection.

> She hated it, she knew how utterly cut off it was, how
> hideous and how sickeningly mindless. Sometimes she
> beat her wings like a new Daphne, turning not into a tree
> but a machine.

Beldover is an underworld, 'strong, dangerous . . . mindless, inhuman.'
And yet the cumulative effect of the novel up to this point has been such
as to enforce the truth that it is through descending into such an underworld that we shall be redeemed. Birkin assures Ursula early on that it is
sensuality he wants, 'that and nothing else at this point':

> It is a fulfilment—the great dark knowledge you can't have
> in your head—the dark involuntary being. It is death to
> one's self—but it is the coming into being of another.'
> 'But how? How can you have knowledge not in your
> head?' she asked, quite unable to interpret his phrases.
> 'In the blood,' he answered; 'when the mind and the
> known world is drowned in darkness—everything must
> go—there must be the deluge. Then you find yourself in a
> palpable body of darkness, a demon—'

The scene from which this is an excerpt will alone have prepared us to
find something of value in the potent and half-repulsive atmosphere of

Beldover. The broad dialect of the mining community is curiously caressing 'to the blood'; the men are *powerful* underworld men who spend most of their time 'in the darkness'. If the 'voluptuous resonance' of this darkness is like that of machinery, and if this use of 'voluptuous' perhaps recalls the 'voluptuous consummation' that Hermione experiences when she endeavours to destroy Birkin with the piece of lapis lazuli (a consummation preceded by the sense that 'darkness' is breaking over her), we may equally be reminded of an earlier episode still and of the 'dark sensual body of life' which Birkin, in passionate disputation, had proposed as an alternative to the life of pure sensation and the bullying will. And after all, Hermione's destructiveness, at that crucial moment, is itself ambivalent. We are told that her mind is a chaos, and the terrible shocks that run over her body, 'like shocks of electricity', assimilate her energy to the nervous and purely reductive energy that Minette and Gerald know. On the other hand, drenched by an involuntary power and drowned in darkness, she is also, at one level, demonic in Birkin's own sense. When he assures her in a letter afterwards,

> You were quite right, to biff me—because I know you wanted to. So there's the end of it . . .

the acknowledgement, given his creed, is no more than her due. On every premise from which this novel proceeds Hermione, released momentarily from the confinements of her own ego ('It was dynamic hatred and loathing, coming strong and black out of the unconsciousness'), must be said to have knowledge at last of sensual reality. What results is horrible enough, but here as elsewhere the effect is to suggest that we must, if we are to be renewed, travel *through* the horror.

And so in Beldover: it is by no means easy to decide just how lethal the lethal-seeming mechanization of the miner's life in fact is. For one thing, the inhumanness and dark callousness of the machine corresponds to a quality of ruthlessness which has already been proposed as no less life-enhancing than life-destructive. There has been this for instance:

> 'Spontaneous! he cried. 'You and spontaneity! You, the most deliberate thing that ever walked or crawled! . . . You want it all in that loathsome little skull of yours, that ought to be cracked like a nut . . .'

Or this:

> She strayed out, pallid and preyed-upon like a ghost,

like one attacked by the tomb-influences which dog us.
And she was gone like a corpse; that has no presence, no
connexion. He remained hard and vindictive.

Or this:

> Gerald watched him closely.
> 'You think we ought to break up this life, just start and
> let fly ?' he asked.
> 'This life. Yes I do. We've got to bust it completely . . .'

The two men don't, of course, mean the same thing by 'break up', or
'bust'; the incipient excitement we sense in Gerald is stirred by a
prospect of *mere* destructiveness, a kind of abandon that is very different
from what Birkin has in mind. But the fact that the two kinds of destructiveness are so unlike while yet being alike is just what is characteristic
of this novel, and just the kind of irony we need to be alert to in the
later passage about Beldover, in the chapter 'Coal-dust'. To begin with,
we note how the strident and mechanical quality of the miner's life is
modified by a deeper and darker rhythm, no less destructive, but far
richer. On the one hand:

> The sense of talk, buzzing, jarring, half-secret, the endless
> mining, and political wrangling, vibrated in the air like
> discordant machinery.

(It is a habit of Lawrence's to convey an impression of impoverished or
merely nervous vitality through images of vibrancy. Hundreds of examples could be supplied. Of Poe's Roderick Usher he writes: 'And the
nerves we know vibrate all the while to unseen presences, unseen forces.
So Roderick Usher quivers on the edge of dissolution'.)[1] But there are
fuller and less discordant notes also.

> Their voices sounded out with strong intonation, and the
> broad dialect was curiously caressing to the blood. It
> seemed to envelope Gudrun in a labourer's caress, there
> was in the whole atmosphere, a resonance of physical men,
> a glamorous thickness of labour and maleness, surcharged
> in the air. But it was universal in the district, and therefore
> unnoticed by the inhabitants. . . .
> Now she realized that this was the world of powerful,
> underworld men who spent most of their time in the
> darkness. In their voices she could hear the voluptuous
> resonance of darkness, the strong, dangerous underworld,
> mindless, inhuman.

This resonance is much closer to what Lawrence called 'the rich centrality of the self'.* We have a sense of involuntary process at the deeper levels of the psyche. And the effect is not merely to indicate the quality of life which the machine is destroying but to invest the mechanical process itself with a paradoxical but genuine vitality.

> It was the same every evening when she came home, she seemed to move through a wave of disruptive force, that was given off from the presence of thousands of vigorous, underworld, half-automatized colliers, and which went to the brain and the heart, awaking a fatal desire, and a fatal callousness. . . .
> They belonged to another world, they had a strange glamour, their voices were full of an intolerable deep resonance, like a machine's burring, a music more maddening that the sirens' long ago.

It is impossible here to dissociate the one resonance from the other.

In one of Lawrence's letters there is a very *un*equivocal passage about the symbolic value of coal and of steel which helps to define, by contrast, the way the language works in the sequence under review from *Women in Love*.

> You are too journalistic, too much concerned with facts. . . .
> Take your Andy . . . What was there in the mines that held

---

* See the first version of the essay on Poe. (In the final version the phrasing is altered to read 'the *true* centrality of the self'.) The fuller or richer resonance is heard again, in a comparable context, in the late essay, *Nottingham and the Mining Country:*

> And the pit did not mechanize men. On the contrary. Under the butty system, the miners worked underground as a sort of intimate community, they knew each other practically naked, and with curious close intimacy, and the darkness and the underground remoteness of the pit 'stall', and the continual presence of danger, made the physical, instinctive, and intuitional contact between men very highly developed, a contact almost as close as touch, very real and very powerful. This physical awareness and intimate *togetherness* was at its strongest down pit. When the men came up into the light, they blinked. They had, in a measure, to change their flow. Nevertheless, they brought with them above ground the curious dark intimacy of the mine, the naked sort of contact, and if I think of my childhood, it is always as if there was a lustrous sort of inner darkness, like the gloss of coal, in which we moved and had our real being.[2]

the boy's feelings? The darkness, the mystery, the other-worldness, the peculiar camaraderie, sort of naked intimacy: men as god in the underworld, or as elementals. Create *that* in a picture.

Then with just a bit of alteration, vivify that middle-part (the best) of your story: steel. Give the mystery, the cruelty, the deathliness of steel, as against the comparative softness, silkiness, naturalness of coal. Throw in that Alice is a symbol of the human ego striving in its vanity, super-ficial: but the man's soul really magnetised by steel, by coal, as two opposing master-elements: carbon versus iron, c and f.

When we get inside ourselves, and away from the vanity of the ego—Alice and smart clothes—then things are symbols. Coal is a symbol of something in the soul, old and dark and silky and natural, and matrix of fire: and steel is a symbol of something else in the soul, hard and death-dealing, cutting, hurting, annihilating the living tissue forever.[3]

In the sequence from 'Coal-Dust', what is old and dark and silky and natural is not to be distinguished as neatly as this from what is hard and death-dealing; for steel seems both to destroy (or half-destroy) the qualities of coal and also to attract those qualities to itself:

> . . . voluptuous resonance of darkness . . . thousands of vigorous, underworld, half-automatized colliers . . . awaking a fatal desire, and a fatal callousness . . . their voices were full of an intolerable deep resonance.

The machine takes over something of the age-old glamour of coal, and its mysterious cruelty is half-sanctioned and half-repudiated. If Gudrun, suffering from her fascination and resisting, is nevertheless compelled by the callousness and disruptiveness, this is a token of her vitality as well as of something worse. And if the colliers are half-automatized, it is also true that the dark, disruptive force which they mediate is an elemental life-energy. And finally, if Ursula is unresponsive to these equivocal resonances, if at this stage in the story she shows no faculty for this knowledge in corruption (effectively she is not present in the scene, though at the beginning we know her to be at Gudrun's side) then so much the worse—as well as the better—for her.

Throughout this commentary I have tended to absorb the concepts of cor-ruption and dis-ruption into each other; and I have done this always with a full sense of being justified by the text. It is as though the phonetic connection alone, and the derivation from a common root (*rumpere*) held for Lawrence its own suggestiveness (the same applies to the phonetic connection between 'reduction' and 'destruction'), setting in motion that process by which more complex and significant kinds of identity-in-difference are linguistically realized. There is, for instance, a real sense in which the 'disruptive force' in Beldover *is* the 'corruptive fire' by virtue of which Birkin annihilates Hermione at Breadalby. But this claim will perhaps carry more conviction if we consider the way the Beldover sequence modulates into the opening paragraphs of 'Sketch Book'.

At the end of 'Coal Dust' we learn how Gudrun makes a practice of strolling the streets with Palmer:

> ... two elegants in one sense: in the other sense, two units, absolutely adhering to the people, teeming with the distorted colliers. . . . All had a secret sense of power, and of inexpressible destructiveness, and of fatal half-heartedness, a sort of rottenness in the will.

And it is precisely a teeming rottenness that holds Gudrun's fascinated attention in the marsh at the end of the lake, to which the scene immediately shifts. Very soon Gerald and Hermione put in their appearance, in a boat.

> And instantly she perished in the keen *frisson* of anticipation, an electric vibration in her veins, intense, much more intense than that which was always humming low in the atmosphere of Beldover.

If life in the underworld of Beldover is voluptuous, dangerous and mindless, so in its own way is this communication between Gudrun and Gerald. Blood, nerves, vibration, voluptuous, power, dangerous, diabolic: all these terms are carried over into the new context. At every level the language insists on the continuity between the dis-ruptive energies of the mining community and the cor-ruptive energies of the marsh. And further, we are no more disposed to a purely negative appraisal or dismissive judgment in this case than we were in the other. I have already observed, apropos of the earlier passage, that Ursula loses as well as gains through her innocence; and this comment is equally relevant to the scene at the lake. While Gudrun is staring at the water-plants, Ursula watches the butterflies, one of them 'breathing with his soft wings, intoxicatingly, breathing pure ethereal sunshine'; and then Ursula rises and drifts away, 'unconscious like the butterflies'. A recent comment on this scene runs as follows:

The butterflies 'are a sign that pure creation takes place'. Their very distinctiveness and selfhood constitutes a heaven of existence, far transcending the uncreate mess of mud from which life struggled all those aeons ago. Gudrun's *nostalgie de la boue* is a symptom of her unconscious desire to lapse back from the struggle for selfhood towards man's first slime.[4]

This response certainly does justice to half, but to only half the poetry. 'She knew how they rose out of the mud', it is said of Gudrun, as she contemplates the water-plants. One recalls how Birkin, copying the Chinese drawing of the geese, 'knows what centres they live from'. In each case there is an acute sensuous vision of corruption, of 'the lotus mystery'.* Later, in the chapter 'Water-Party', Birkin assures Ursula that

> Aphrodite is born in the first spasm of universal dissolution
> —then the snakes and swans and lotus—marsh-flowers—
> and Gudrun and Gerald—born in the process of destruc-
> tive creation.

In the 'Sketch Book' episode Gerald's hand comes 'straight forward like a stem'. Moreover, his body surges 'like the marsh-fire' (an analogue of the 'corruptive fire' that Birkin intuitively discovers 'in the flux of cold water and mud') and this reminds us of the surging water-plants. But these plants are not only surging; they are 'rigid, naked', 'thick and cool and fleshy'. The ooze is the source of an evident phallic energy. One thinks of 'Nilus' slime' in *Antony and Cleopatra*; and indeed if there is a novel in the language which can be said to be close in spirit to Shakespeare's play it is *Women in Love*. Neither Shakespeare nor Lawrence pretends that the slime into which his lovers descend is less than degrad-

---

* Compare this, from 'The Two Principles', *English Review*, June 1919:

> In the face we live our glad life of seeing, perceiving, we pass in delight to our greater being, when we are one with all things. The face and breast belong to the heavens, the luminous infinite. But in the loins we have our unbreakable root, the *root of the lotus*. There we have our passionate self-possession, our unshakable and indomitable being. There deep calls unto deep. There in the sexual passion the very blood surges into communication, in the terrible sensual oneing. There all the darkness of the deeps, the primal flood, is perfected, as the two great waves of separated blood surge to consummation, the dark infinitude. (*Italics mine.*)

ing; yet in both the novel and the play the slime generates and sustains erotic life.

Once again it is worth invoking the argument of *The Crown*.

> The snake is the spirit of the great corruptive principle, the festering cold of the marsh. This is how he seems, as we look back. We revolt from him, but we share the same life and tide of life as he. He struggles as we struggle, he enjoys the sun, as he comes to the water to drink, he curls up, hides himself to sleep. And under the low skies of the far past aeons, he emerged a king out of chaos, a long beam of new life. But the vulture looms out in sleep like a rock, invincible against the flux of both eternities.

The phrase 'festering cold' (we note how much is done here to complicate the normal emotive impact of 'festering') virtually recurs in 'Sketch-Book', where the theme once more is the 'festering chill' of the marsh, the great corruptive principle. It need hardly be said that of the two texts the fictional one is incomparably the denser. Here again, as in the passage about Beldover, the thin resonance suggestive of pure nervous excitement contends with a much fuller resonance. On the one hand there is this:

> And instantly she perished in the keen *frisson* of anticipation . . . He seemed to stoop to something. His glistening, whitish hair seemed like the electricity of the sky . . . An intensification of pride went over his nerves.

('Glistening', with its thin vowel-sound, is a favourite word of Lawrence's in this kind of context and is used of Gerald on a number of occasions.) On the other hand there is this:

> Gudrun, absorbed in a stupor of apprehension of surging water-plants, sat crouched on the shoal, drawing, not looking up for a long time, and then staring unconsciously, absorbedly at the rigid, naked, succulent stems. . . .
> And as if in a spell, Gudrun was aware of his body, stretching and surging like the marsh-fire, stretching towards her, his hand coming straight forward like a stem. Her voluptuous, acute apprehension of him made the blood faint in her veins, her mind went dim and unconscious. And he rocked on the water perfectly, like the rocking of phosphorescence. He looked round at the boat. It was drifting off a little. He lifted the oar to bring it back. And the exquisite pleasure of slowly arresting the boat, in the heavy-soft water, was complete as a swoon.

There is a good deal here that tells against the lovers; and yet Gudrun's capacity to lose herself in contemplation, 'like a Buddhist' (in sharp contrast to the unflagging egoism of Hermione), Gerald's assimilation to the surging organic energies of the marsh, and that final image of plenitude, of resting or calmly riding on an unexcited natural force, argues for a valuable life going on below the level of the ego or the will.

In *The Savage Pilgrimage* Catherine Carswell gives the following account of a conversation she had with Lawrence after she had read the MS. of *Women in Love:*

> I had not only a wholesome fear of Lawrence. I was shy, and even suspicious of most of the friends by whom he was now surrounded. I did not fit well with them, and there was something in their relation with him that saddened me. If he needed them, then he did, and it was his affair. But I got the feeling that he did not think much of them, and was using them for what he needed, not so much willingly as *malgré lui.*
>
> It was from his experience with these friends, and their interrelations through Frieda, that he wrote *Women in Love*. Later, when he gave me the MS. of that novel to read, I asked him why must he write of people who were so far removed from the general run, people so sophisticated and 'artistic' and spoiled, that it could hardly matter what they did or said? To which he replied that it was only through such people that one could discover whither the general run of mankind, the great unconscious mass, was tending. There, at the uttermost tips of the flower of an epoch's achievement, one could already see the beginning of the flower of putrefaction which must take place before the seed of the new was ready to fall clear. I gathered too that in the nature of the putrefaction the peculiar nature of an epoch was revealed. And the more quickly we recognized and accepted the nature of the failure, the more speedily would the new unknown seed find a condition for its germination. Achievement carried to its furthest limits coincided with putrefaction. Those who sought the new must take their stand right in the flux.

This image of the untainted observer (the artist is doomed to take his stand within the putrefaction but is not part of it) is a shaping force in *Women in Love* from beginning to end. But equally important, at the very least, is the notion that we are *all* of us caught up in the mud (inevitably, since our culture is in its death-throes) and further, that there is virtue in the mud; it is the source of new life. We do not know how accurately Catherine Carswell recovered the crucial phrases ('I am not now reporting Lawrence's actual words, which I cannot remember, but I use remembered phrases to give the impression he conveyed—an impression familiar to all his readers') but it is interesting to observe that the image of putrescence in flower does justice to both the kinds of vitality that I have been considering in the foregoing pages: namely, the organic and the reductive. The flower is a flower *of* putrefaction. But also its blooming is a moment in the organic cycle. There might appear to be no such fusion of organic and reductive in the corresponding passage in 'Water-Party'; it is the inverse process that the *fleurs du mal* are a product of, and the notion that this is at the same time a necessary life-process seems muted. But in fact the notion is by no means as muted as the initial disjunction between the rivers of life and corruption would seem to suggest.

> 'Some people are pure flowers of dark corruption—lilies.
> But there ought to be some roses, warm and flamy . . .'

It is not proposed that there ought to be nothing but roses. Clearly 'corruption' doesn't have the kind of impact here that it has, for example, in this passage from *The Crown:*

> But childhood as a *goal*, for which grown people aim: childishness futile and sentimental, for which men and women lust, and which always retreats when grasped, like the *ignis fatuus* of a poisonous marsh of corruption: this is disgusting.

The substance of Birkin's complaint is not so much that we belong to the death-process as that we belong to it entirely; there are two realities —the demonic and the paradisal—and today we know only one of them. This, at all events, is what he is saying on one level. Yet he also hints at the possibility that there *is* only one river after all—the river of corruption—and that the other is merely a myth. I shall be returning to this point. The relevant comment to make at the moment is that the passage illustrates the habit of Lawrence's which I began by considering: a relatively simple attitude to corruption is overlaid by an attitude that is anything but simple. A certain limited scope is allowed for a moralistic reading, a mild revulsion from 'the snakes and swans and lotus'. But there are good reasons also for discounting such a reading; as usual, Lawrence has his cake and eats it too.

The role played in the novel by the wood-carvings from the West Pacific, or Africa,* confirms, I think, the reading which I have so far offered; that is, justifies one in being unwilling to take the concepts of disruption, corruption, destruction and so on simply at their face value. The sensuality that the wood-carvings embody is certainly reductive, but just as certainly the response they provoke in the reader is or ought to be far from simple or undivided. Yet the following commentary has been offered recently by George Ford:

> That the African statues signify for Birkin a whole process of decline and fall, and that however aesthetically pleasing they evoke for him the impurity of a degenerated civilization are points I have been laboring partly because of an extraordinary discussion of these statues by Horace Gregory in his *Pilgrim of the Apocalypse*. According to Gregory, Lawrence found his principal characters of less interest than the statue of the West African woman, 'for him, perhaps the most important figure in the book'.
>
>> She is positive, concrete, the perfect representative of life as opposed to the imperfect human beings surrounding her . . . What the statue is made to represent is the *normal* essence of Gudrun and Ursula combined—their deviation from the statue's norm . . . is the perversion imposed upon them by their individual existence . . . In all four characters, male and female, the statue sets the standard, never fully realized by any of them.
>
> And Mr. Gregory concludes his analysis by asserting that 'the image of the West African savage' was a fragment of hope in the midst of death.

Professor Ford is amazed that so perceptive a critic should have gone so 'fantastically wrong'. Yet Gregory is responding to significances that are certainly there. Birkin considers the statue at Halliday's to be representative of an 'awful pitch of culture, of a definite sort':

> Pure culture in sensation, culture in the physical consciousness, really ultimate *physical* consciousness, mindless, utterly sensual. It is so sensual as to be final, supreme!

Gerald objects: 'You like the wrong things, Rupert . . . things against yourself'. And Birkin replies, 'Oh, I know, this isn't everything'—an

---

* In the original version, they were all from the West Pacific; Lawrence made a partial and slightly confusing adjustment because of the threat of a libel action by Heseltine, the original of Halliday, who is the owner of the carvings in the novel.

avowal, by implication, that at any rate it is, and positively, something. True, we learn that the face is 'terrible' and that Gerald 'saw Minette in it'. But this only confirms with special sharpness the way Lawrence's art here turns the screw on the reader: we cannot blink the fact that it is the face of a savage and abstracted almost into meaningless, and yet we must hold in the mind at the same time the suggestion that this is a condition of being that has marked affinities with the kind of sensuality which has already been proposed as redemptive. 'Beyond the limits of mental consciousness, mindless, utterly sensual': it is impossible not to recall Birkin's 'great dark knowledge you can't have in your head—the dark involuntary being'. But the early argument with Hermione which led Birkin to attest his beliefs has at the same time prepared the reader for discriminations between *kinds* of sensual knowledge: we are not to confuse 'actual sensual being' on the one hand and 'vicious mental deliberate profligacy' on the other.

> . . . you want to go back and be like a savage, without knowledge. You want a life of pure sensation and 'passion'. . .

is the charge Birkin brings against Hermione. The distinctions which Birkin makes explicitly here in the class-room are established in the Soho episodes more deviously. First, the wood-carving conveys 'the suggestion of the extreme of physical sensation'; it is 'pure culture in sensation'. Then we learn that Minette, with the 'inchoate look of a violated slave', makes Gerald's nerves 'quiver with acutely desirable sensation'; 'he tingled with the subtle, biting sensation'. And then the Arab, 'half a savage', puts in his appearance again, his face 'immutable, aristocratic-looking, tinged slightly with grey under the skin' (Compare: 'He saw vividly with his spirit the *grey* forward-stretching face of the savage woman') and we register the reaction of Birkin:

> But Birkin felt a slight sickness, looking at him, and feeling the slight greyness as an ash or a corruption, in the aristocratic inscrutability of expression a nauseating, bestial stupidity.

The effect of it all is clear enough: actual sensual being is one thing, the attempt to recover sensuality through the will, having it all in the consciousness—sophisticating the savage—is quite another. We cannot go back; on the other hand we have to find our own *equivalent* of the savage mindlessness. We need to recover the capacity for knowledge in the blood, the dark unknowingness.

But now a distinction needs to be made, for the African fetish which forms the subject of Birkin's relections in the chapter 'Moony' does not have the same significance as the earlier figure of the woman in labour. This passage in 'Moony' is perhaps the most difficult in the novel, and I shall need to approach it circuitously.

Towards the end of the novel there is a curious if minor reversal of roles; whereas earlier Birkin had been presented as the more innocent of the two men, at the end the innocence, by implication, is attributed to Gerald. In the chapter 'Man to Man' we get this:

> Gerald listened with a faint, fine smile on his face, all the time, as if, somewhere, he knew so much better than Birkin, all about this . . .

And again:

> Gerald looked at Birkin with subtle eyes of knowledge. But he would never openly admit what he felt. He knew more than Birkin, in one direction—much more. And this gave him his gentle love for the other man, as if Birkin were in some way young, innocent, child-like; so amazingly clever, but incurably innocent.

This looks forward to 'Moony'—'She knew what he himself [i.e. Birkin] did not know'—and it is borne out very soon by the episode involving Gerald, Gudrun and the rabbit: 'they were implicated with each other in abhorent mysteries'. And yet towards the end it is Birkin who has to explain Loerke's significance to Gerald, whose earlier capacity for subtle knowledge in corruption seems to some extent to have deserted him.

> 'I don't understand your terms, really,' he said in a flat, doomed voice. 'But it sounds a rum sort of desire.'
> 'I suppose we want the same,' said Birkin. 'Only we want to take a quick jump downwards, in a sort of ecstasy— and he ebbs with the stream, the sewer stream'.

Of course Birkin has always been the more articulate of the two; still, in the Gerald of the last act there really is a touch of what Gudrun complains of in him—he is just a little of a *Dummkopf*. 'But it sounds a rum sort of desire': this is almost the obtuse, clean-limbed, athletic Englishman! But the reason for this toning down is clear enough; a distinction needs to be drawn between Gerald's limited perversity and Loerke's far subtler capacities.

> How should Gerald hope to satisfy a woman of Gudrun's calibre ? . . .
> . . . She had further to go, a farther, slow, exquisite experience to reap, unthinkable subtleties of sensation to know, before she was finished.

'Unthinkable subtleties': we are taken back to Birkin's reflections on the African fetish—'sensual subtle realities far beyond the scope of phallic investigation'.

The distinction between Gerald and Loerke crystallizes a distinction which has been implicit throughout the novel. The disintegrative processes are beautiful, and also obscene. Gerald embodies the beauty, the phosphorescence of decay, and Loerke the obscenity, the reduction of the sensual self to inorganic chaos. (There is Loerke as well as Gerald in Poe, who is a master of the *'inorganic* consciousness'.)[5] This distinction is too schematic of course, but I have drawn it in order to make a point about the African fetish. The attitude to the fetish (and to disintegration and corruption) in that passage in 'Moony' is for the most part the attitude appropriate to Loerke; the *beauty* of the reductive process is virtually denied throughout. But, as so often in poetry, the effect of this denial of a meaning is that the meaning denied asserts itself quietly as a positive value: we have a sense that there are considerations that are not being taken into account.

> . . . the desire for creation and productive happiness must have lapsed, leaving the single impulse for knowledge in one sort, mindless progressive knowledge through the senses . . . mystic knowledge in disintegration and dissolution.

To accept these disjunctions as final would be to reject Birkin's own creed of sensual fulfilment, for on his own showing it is through a kind of dissolution and corruption that we come to know 'sensual reality'. True, the dissolution that will bring us new life is not that of the beetle-faced savage; on the other hand the two kinds of dissolution have very significant affinities.

Women in Love in effect 'affirms' both these propositions more or less continuously; holiness is quite other than degradation, and also is nourished by degradation. In the passage under immediate review it is the disjunction of the two, the antipathy, we are largely conscious of. Yet how can this antipathy fail to be secretly and very significantly qualified when the novel has done so much to confirm that there is a beauty and vitality in putrescence, and in the reductive process generally? What does the chapter 'Water Party' say if not that the flux of corruption, or the process of living disintegration (to use again the language of the essay on Poe) is 'slow and bitter and beautiful, too'?

> Her soul was really pierced with beauty, she was translated beyond herself. . . . And they stood together in one luminous union, close together and ringed round with light, all the rest excluded.
> . . . Then he clambered into the boat. Oh, and the beauty of the subjection of his loins, white and dimly luminous as he climbed over the side of the boat, his back rounded and soft—ah, this was too much for her, too final a vision. She knew it, and it was fatal. The terrible hopelessness of fate, and of beauty, such beauty!
> He was not like a man to her, he was an incarnation, a great phase of life.

This last passage is not perhaps one of the most successful in the book, but it must be conceded that by this point Lawrence has at any rate earned the *right* to the lyricism. 'A great phase of *life*': it is not only the beauty but the inverse vitality of the reductive process that his language has consistently realized.

To return then to 'Moony': a careful reader will not be prepared to go all the way with Birkin when he repudiates 'the putrescent mystery of sun rays'; nor will he suppose that this rejection is decisive and final. And indeed almost immediately the truths that have been obscured during Birkin's reflections re-assert themselves. On the strength of his conclusion that the African way is to be categorically rejected Birkin goes off to propose to Ursula: 'He thought of Ursula, how sensitive and delicate she really was. . . .' But the proposal is a fiasco and he makes directly for Shortlands, and Gerald. The two men engage in a wrestling match, committing themselves so utterly in the combat as to go 'beyond the limits of mental consciousness', like the savage woman in labour.

> It was as if Birkin's whole *physical intelligence* inter-penetrated into Gerald's body, as if his fine, sublimated energy entered into the flesh of the fuller man, like some potency, casting a fine net, a prison, through the muscles into the very depths of Gerald's *physical being*.

This, as in the case of the woman in labour, is 'ultimate *physical* consciousness, mindless, utterly sensual'.

> The earth seemed to tilt and sway, and a complete

> darkness was coming over his mind. He did not know
> what happened.

This dissolution in violence is clearly a good deal closer to knowledge in corruption than to 'goodness, holiness and the desire for creation and productive happiness'. The experience the men share, it is fair to say, is equivalent to that mystical death which the Africans must have undergone 'thousands of years' ago, when 'the relations between the senses and the outspoken mind' broke, 'leaving the experience all in one sort, mystically sensual' (though the *ugliness* of mindless knowledge is underscored in the earlier context in a way it isn't here). At all events, after reading 'Gladiatorial' (and 'Excurse') we are likely to be that much more sensitive to the full significance of the passage in 'Moony', readier to recognize that the African knowledge is mindless in a positive as well as a negative sense. True, the novel has been educating us in this special kind of perceptiveness from the first chapter. On the other hand, in 'Moony' the sheer horror of the dreadful African mysteries is so insisted on that we need to be unusually alert if we are to recognize that 'mystery', 'mystic' and 'mystical' are also pointing, obscurely, to something desirable: a quality of intense non-mental spirituality; the mystic's capacity for a saving knowledge-beyond-knowledge. And it is sensual mysticism in this positive mode that becomes a theme for praise in 'Excurse', praise darkly hinted at where the associations were with African savagery, but now explicit and unqualified.

> . . . vital, sensual reality that can never be transmuted
> into mind content . . . the *mystic* body of reality.

and:

> Darkness and silence must fall perfectly on her, then she
> could know *mystically*, in unrevealed touch. She must
> lightly, mindlessly connect with him, have the knowledge
> which is death of knowledge, the reality of surety in not
> knowing.

In short, 'mystically sensual', in the passage in 'Moony', has the force of an oxymoron. The sensuality ends in the senses—is 'arrested'; yet it also leads into the unknown.* To say this however is very different from

---

* Compare my argument, above, that in effect there are two Anton Skrebenskys—the mere sensualist and the sensual mystic, one of them capable of leading into the unknown and the other not. But here, in *Women in Love*, the tension between these two modes of sensuality does not affect us as sheer inconsistency, as in the Skrebensky sequences it too often does.

observing that the carved African woman, because mystically sensual, expresses 'an ideal unity of body and mind . . . achieved through "disintegration and dissolution" of old-fashioned ideals like goodness, holiness, happiness and the desire for creation'.[6] For in fact these old-fashioned ideals are affirmed very positively, and what we are confronted with throughout are antinomies—not an 'ideal unity' or a resolution of opposites.

And this is true of the novel as a whole. Leavis has spoken of 'the "spontaneous-creative fullness of being" out of which *Women in Love* comes'.[7] It is a way of making his point that has probably proved quite as harmful as corrective. For it tends to imply—whether what is in question, primarily, is the artefact or the endowment of the artificer—that the only impulses that make for health or wholeness are the pure, creative impulses. (It is in keeping with this attitude that Leavis should affirm, without any qualification, that 'The West African statuette . . . represents something that we are to see as a default, a failure'.*) 'The creative-*destructive* fulness of being out of which *Women in Love* comes' would be a happier way of putting it.

* See above p. xiv.

III Women in Love: *Individuality and belonging*

That self-sufficiency should entail belonging is an irony realized in the poetry of the English Romantics (especially the poetry of Wordsworth) again and again; to admit the necessity of the bond with Nature is to make possible a true integrity. And we note that in Lawrence's fiction likewise, and particularly in *Women in Love*, singleness can only come to pass with the acknowledgement of community and with the disintegration of the hard and isolate ego. It is this irony I shall largely be concerned with in the present chapter. My theme is not individuality merely but *kinds* of individuality, *kinds* of integration and disintegration (and, as a corollary, kinds of dissolution and corruption).

The actual word 'disintegration' is used frequently in *Women in Love* and almost always with a negative force; and this no doubt accounts in part for the common assumption that throughout the novel the disintegrative processes are conceived of as purely life-destructive. The following reading is representative:[1]

> Gerald's work in the mines and Gudrun's art are revealed as 'disintegrative', as an abuse of organic life; and the black sensuality of their relationship is productive of the violence which, in the novel, is seen as an inevitable concomitant of *any* process of 'dissolution'.* (Italics mine).

* Compare also, from the same critic, H. M. Daleski:
> The recurrence of the phrase 'disintegration and dissolution' —it is the key motive of the book, indicative of a general

If my argument in the previous chapters is sound, this will not do. For the organic is not the only kind of life that counts in *Women in Love*, nor is violence there merely destructive. And the process of dissolution is positive quite as often as not, or positive-negative; the coming into being of the true and 'original individuality of the blood' entails a dissolving, or disintegrating, of the 'dreary individuality of the ego'.[2]

The structure of this irony can be traced with special ease in the following passage from the *Letters*:

> I am so sick of people: they preserve an evil, bad, separating spirit under the warm cloak of good words. That is intolerable in them. . . . They all want the same thing: a continuing in this state of disintegration wherein each separate little ego is an independent little principality by itself. What does Russell really want? He wants to keep his own established ego, his finite and ready-defined self intact, free from contact and connection. He wants to be ultimately a free agent. That is what they all want, ultimately—that is what is at the back of all international peace-for-ever and democratic control talks they want an outward system of nullity, which they call peace and goodwill, so that in their own souls they can be independent little gods, referred nowhere and to nothing, little mortal Absolutes, secure from question.[4]

Though Russell and Co. live and want to continue in a state of vicious disintegration—the body politic fragmented, reduced to component particles—it is, by implication, only some process of disintegration which can rescue them. For how is each to establish contact and connection again if not by the dissolution of his independent little principality—the hard, separate ego? In other words the disintegrated state is at the same time a state of false integrity, implying as it does a fatal intactness of the established, finite self. Only through a submission to disintegration can the disintegrated condition be superseded.

As I have implied, it is a token of Lawrence's Romantic lineage that his diagnosis of false integrity should be so bound up with the theme of belonging.

---

process against which Birkin and Ursula pit themselves—
. . . takes us back to the whirlpool of the Pompadour.[3]

Daleski has a clear perception that Lawrence sees the need 'for both firm singleness and melting union'; and yet the corollary—that in these circumstances it is most unlikely that disintegration will have for Lawrence an unequivocal negative value—escapes his attention.

> He was alone now, alone and immune in the middle of the waters, which he had all to himself. He exulted in his isolation in the new element, unquestioned and un-conditioned. He was happy, thrusting with his legs and all his body, without bond or connexion anywhere, just himself in the watery world.
>
> Gudrun envied him almost painfully. Even this momentary possession of pure isolation and fluidity seemed to her so terribly desirable that she felt herself as if damned, out there on the high-road.

On the face of it the language might appear to endorse Gerald's perfect immunity and apparent self-sufficiency. But a separateness that goes with an exultant sense of one's own advantage and entails sheer mobility and fluidity, no bond or connexion of any kind, can only be suspect. This equating of fluidity and dissolution—a dissolving of the bonds that ought to link an individual to his human and natural environment—begins very early in the novel and is sustained throughout.

In the episode in question separateness is not opposed to the dissolved condition but entails it. In the following instance on the other hand the process of dissolution, though painful and nauseating, is on the whole a sign of life, a sign that here is a human spirit in contact with the rhythms of living and dying. The incapacity to dissolve or be transmuted, by contrast, is conceived of as a mark of the isolated and mechanical state.

> In a kind of spiritual trance, she yielded, she gave way, and all was dark. She could feel, within the darkness, the terrible assertion of her body, the unutterable anguish of dissolution, the only anguish that is too much, the far-off awful nausea of dissolution set in within the body.
>
> 'Does the body correspond so immediately with the spirit?' she asked herself. And she knew, with the clarity of ultimate knowledge, that the body is only one of the manifestations of the spirit, the transmutation of the integral spirit is the transmutation of the physical body as well. Unless I set my will, unless I absolve myself from the rhythm of life, fix myself and remain static, cut off from living, absolved within my own will. But better die than live mechanically a life that is a repetition of repeti-tions. To die is to move on with the invisible. To die is also a joy, a joy of submitting to that which is greater than the known; namely, the pure unknown. That is a joy. But to live mechanized and cut off within the motion of the will,

to live as an entity absolved from the unknown, that is shameful and ignominious. There is no ignominy in death. There is complete ignominy in an unreplenished, mechanized life.

The truly integral spirit then preserves its integrity both by its resistance to dissolution and by its aptness to dissolve; and true individuality is a matter of belonging. But the distinction made in previous chapters between paradisal and reductive vitality is relevant here also; for belonging may or may not entail the acknowledging within oneself—and the incorporating—of corruption. On the one hand it is precisely in terms of corruption or putrescence that Lawrence is apt to image the mechanized or cut-off state (I quote from one of the later essays):

> And this, this desire, is the reality which is inside love.
> The ego itself plays a false part in it. The individual is like
> a deep pool, or tarn, in the mountains, fed from beneath
> by unseen springs, and having no obvious inlet or outlet.
> The springs which feed the individual at the depths are
> sources of power, power from the unknown. . . .
> Our education goes on and on, on and on, making the
> sexes alike, destroying the original individuality of the
> blood, to substitute for it this dreary individuality of the
> ego, the Number One. Out of the ego streams neither
> Blue Nile nor White Nile. The infinite number of little
> human egos make a mosquito marsh, where nothing
> happens except buzzing and biting, ooze and degeneration.
> . . . Don Juan was only Don Juan because he *had* no real
> desire. He had broken his own integrity, and was a mess
> to start with. No stream of desire, with a course of its own,
> flowed from him. He was a marsh in himself.

But put this, from the essay . . . *Love Was Once A Little Boy*, beside some of the passages I have already quoted from *The Crown* or *The Reality of Peace:*

> Corruption will at last break down for us the deadened
> forms, and release us into the infinity.

> We must know that we, ourselves, are the living stream
> of seething corruption, this also, all the while, as well as
> the bright river of life. We must recover our balance to
> be free. From our bodies comes the issue of corruption as
> well as the issue of creation.

It is by means of corruption that we destroy spurious integrity; yet this spurious integrity differs from true integrity as the corruption of a marsh from the purity of a mountain stream.

But this double attitude of Lawrence's is not surprising when seen in its historical context; for it only reflects a doubleness in the Romantic tradition itself. In Europe and Russia in the nineteenth century (one thinks particularly of Dostoievsky) prose fiction and poetry alike paid full tribute to the notion that 'we, ourselves, are the living stream of seething corruption'. The complementary notion that we are also a bright river of life, fed from beneath by unseen springs, is especially characteristic of *English* Romanticism.

Coleridge's *Dejection: An Ode* will serve as an example of the paradisal tradition. It deals not merely with solitariness but with *kinds* of solitariness, obliquely inviting comparison between these kinds in such a way as to generate a sort of irony. On the one hand it is concerned with isolation and the horror of not belonging, and on the other with self-sufficiency, a condition imaged by the crescent moon, 'as fixed as if it grew In its own cloudless, starless lake of blue'. It has been justly remarked, concerning lines 21–38, that Coleridge, 'searching for relief within himself,

> . . . finds it in the rhythm of his stanza as he rises through images of solemn calm and friendly movement to contemplate the perfect self-centredness and self-illuminating of the lotus-like moon. More continuously than any other writer, Coleridge had admired Milton, the poet whose 'self-possession' enabled him to 'attract all forms and things to himself'.[6]

This self-possession or self-sufficiency is the very reverse of isolation.

> A sweet and potent voice, of its own birth,
> Of all sweet sounds the life and element!

Though self-born and self-sustaining, joy is a token of involvement:

> To her may all things live, from pole to pole,
> Their life the eddying of her living soul!

The metaphor of the eddy 'implies a ceaseless and circular interchange of life between soul and nature in which it is impossible to distinguish what is given from what is received'.[7] And this radiating of life which is at the same time a receiving, this independence that is equally a belonging, is the mark of the pure in heart:

Joy, virtuous Lady! Joy that ne'er was given
Save to the pure, and in their purest hour.

Making allowances for obvious differences, we recognize here the positives of ... *Love Was Once A Little Boy*—purity, innocence, at-one-ness—or of a comparable passage in the essay, *John Galsworthy:*

> While a man remains a man, before he falls and becomes a social individual, he innocently feels himself altogether within the great continuum of the universe. He is not divided nor cut off. Men may be against him, the tide of affairs may be rising to sweep him away. But he is one with the living continuum of the universe ...
>
> Lear was essentially happy, even in his greatest misery. A happiness from which Goneril and Regan were excluded as lice and bugs are excluded from happiness, being social beings, and, as such, parasites, fallen from true freedom and independence.[8]

As in *Dejection* true independence or individuality is seen to be a question of belonging. And what is more, it is the symptom and the expression of an essential purity or naïveté. Coleridge opposes purity to sensuality and pride, Lawrence opposes naïveté to social-consciousness and money-consciousness; but these differences are less remarkable than the resemblances.

And the resemblances would have been no less striking if for purposes of illustration we had chosen Wordsworth's *Resolution and Independence*. On the one hand there are the poet's apprehensions about solitude and poverty and on the other the equanimity of the ancient leech-gatherer, a presence at once spectral and substantial, solitary and self-contained: the fear of loneliness and the fact of aloneness in arresting contiguity. A true Child of earth, the leech-gatherer forms part of the natural scene in the way a huge rock does, or a sea-beast. He belongs and yet exists by himself. The poet on the other hand, before his strange encounter, is in very much that spiritual condition which Lawrence defines in the essay on Galsworthy:

> But if man loses his mysterious naïve assurance, which is his innocence; if he gives *too* much importance to the external objective reality and so collapses in his natural innocent pride, then he becomes obsessed with the idea of objectives or material assurance; he wants to *insure* himself, and perhaps everybody else; universal insurance. The impulse rests on fear.

The poet's freely-voiced anxieties—'How is it that you live, and what is it you do?'—are utterly foreign to the leech-gatherer, poor though he is, and his equanimity remains unshaken: 'Housing, with God's good help, by choice or chance; and in this way he gained an honest maintenance'. In short the poem leads up very directly to that dignified moralistic ending. The leech-gatherer's example has both shamed the poet and reassured him: what kills fear is 'the essential innocence and naïveté of the human being, the sense of being at one with the great universe-continuum of space-time-life'.

The poem turns then on an unstated play upon possible senses of 'lonely', a word the poet comes back to again and again as he reads into the old man's condition his own unreasoning fears. ('Yet it befell that, in this *lonely* place', 'This is a *lonesome* place for one like you', 'While he was talking thus, the *lonely* place', 'Wandering about *alone* and silently', 'I'll think of the leech-gatherer on the *lonely* moor!') The leech-gatherer can scarcely be said even to comprehend these fears: 'Ere he replied, a flash of mild *surprise* Broke from the sable orbs of his yet-vivid eyes'. In fact, with his cheerfulness, courtesy and firmness of mind he robs the word 'lonely' not only of its terror but of its very relevance or meaning; we are persuaded that the appropriate word for his condition is not loneliness but independence.

It has been argued that the Romantic artist wrests a paradoxical joy and poetry itself out of his anguish and isolation;[9] but in the poems under review isolation is quite simply the enemy of joy and by no sort of ingenuity or paradox can they be reconciled. The Coleridge of *Dejection* does not regard his anguish as a mark of privilege, as Keats and Yeats do, nor as being in any sense the source of poetry. The version in the letter to Sotheby makes it clear that the true poet, Wordsworth, is not isolated but self-sufficient.

> Calm steadfast Spirit, guided from above,
> O Wordsworth! . . .

> Thus, thus doest thou rejoice.
> To thee do all things live from pole to pole.

Isolation is the lot of the 'sensual and proud', the Goneril and Regan of Lawrence's essay, or of 'the poor loveless ever-anxious crowd' to which, at bottom, the poet in his present condition surely feels himself to belong. If, estranged and sick in mind, he nevertheless creates the present poem, it is with the energy of repudiation that he does so and through embracing imaginatively a condition of health. Similarly the calm and joy at the conclusion of *Resolution and Independence* are not won paradoxically from isolation but from a recognition that what had seemed isolation to the apprehensive inner eye, contemplating the situation of the aged leech-gatherer, is in fact self-sufficiency, and this discovery destroys the observer's *own* isolation, or fear of it. At the end of the poem he becomes once more, by implication, a happy Child of earth.

The Ancient Mariner is the obvious choice to illustrate the alternative tradition. It is significant that it is in a poem about a snake and a visitation from the dangerous underworld that Lawrence should mention the albatross: in recalling the bird and its slaying he is also recalling in effect the blessing of the water-snakes and the role played by demons and witches. The horror in both poems, surely, has sexual implications ('A sort of horror, a sort of protest against his withdrawing into that horrid black hole') and in both poems the denial of demonic life is a source of guilt ('And I have something to expiate'). It ought not to need emphasizing that in appending a moral as he did Coleridge falsified the spirit of his tale, as he recognized himself in his remark to Mrs Barbault. Though the blessing of the water-snakes is ostensibly an act of love—'A spring of love gushed from my heart'—it is not love in the sense suggested by the notorious stanza at the end. To love 'all things both great and small' is a comfortably general requirement and sounds easy, especially if the objects of our love are to be harmless and appealing creatures like the albatross. But at the climax of the poem it is not the albatross but the water-snakes that are blessed, and these point back to the slimy things that crawled 'with legs Upon the slimy sea'.

> About, about, in reel and rout
> The death-fires danced at night;
> The water like a witch's oils,
> Burnt green, and blue and white.

This surely is remembered later:

> Within the shadow of the ship
> I watched their rich attire:
> Blue, glossy green, and velvet black
> They coiled and swam; and every track
> Was a flash of golden fire.

Not only are the colours remembered—green and blue—but 'coiled' recalls 'About, about, in reel and rout' and also perhaps, through the

sound-link, 'oils'; while 'golden fire' is reminiscent of 'death-fires' and
'burnt'. In blessing the water-snakes the mariner is accepting not merely
the creatures that move 'in tracks of shining white' but the rotting sea,
the slimy things, and the witches' oils; accepting the demonic in short,
as Lawrence does in *Snake*. Belonging, then, is a radically different
matter in *The Ancient Mariner* from what it is in *Dejection*; in the
mariner's universe a man only becomes self-sufficient or self-possessed
(in the sense already defined) by accepting what his quotidian consciousness, too often, finds repulsive. This of course is essentially the reading
that Maud Bodkin, applying Jungian categories, proposed in *Archetypal
Patterns in Poetry:*

> In his discussion of Progression and Regression, as 'fun-
> damental concepts of the libido-theory', Jung describes
> progression as 'the daily advance of the process of
> psychological adaptation', which, at certain times, fails.
> Then 'the vital feeling' disappears; there is a damming up
> of energy—of libido. At such times, in the patients he has
> studied, neurotic symptoms are observed, and repressed
> contents appear, of inferior and unadapted character.
> 'Slime out of the depths' he calls such contents . . . but
> slime that contains not only 'objectionable animal
> tendencies, but also germs of new possibilities of life'.
>   Such an ambivalent character in the slimy things,
> glowing and miscreate, Coleridge seems to have felt
> through the travellers' tales, and wrought into expressive-
> ness in his magical picture of the creatures of the calm,
> which the Mariner first despised and then accepted with
> love, to his own salvation. Before 'a renewal of life' can
> come about, Jung urges, there must be an acceptance of
> the possibilities that lie in the unconscious contents
> 'activated through regression . . . and disfigured by the
> slime of the deep'.*

It is a reading that does not appear to have commended itself at all
widely, to judge from more recent commentaries. Thus Professor H. W.
Piper, agreeing with Humphrey House that the moral of the poem is
'He Prayeth best who loveth best . . .', remarks:

> It is our joy in the beauty of the world that enables us to
> love the Law that governs it. As Wordsworth put it, and

* The quotes from Jung are taken from *Contributions to Analytical
Psychology*, Kegan Paul, 1928, pp. 34–40.

as one may interpolate from what he and Coleridge believed,
those whose hearts have been kept pure by the imagination,
and who submit themselves to nature, will find in the world
a strange beauty, that will lead them to love all life and all
the living world. . . .*

Clearly this stress on purity leaves little room for the notion that the
mariner's acceptance of corruption is so inward that his salvation may,
in an important sense, be said to emerge *from* the corruption. An affirmation akin to Wordsworth's is of course there in the poem, but it includes
its own antithesis.

In *Women in Love* as in *The Ancient Mariner* corruption is both
equated with and stands over against a static and deadly isolation. But
whereas Ursula suffers her isolation under the moon, a moon conceived
of as brilliantly and repellently hard,† the mariner suffers under a glaring
sun and a copper sky, while the moon witnesses his regeneration—or
partial regeneration. The luminosity and glory which it projects is
essentially that which the poet aspires to in *Dejection*, a 'beautiful and
beauty-making power' that can transform the whole appearance of the
natural world; what is imaged, in other words, by the moon's light-
giving power and easy self-propulsion is the state of self-possession or
self-sufficiency. And as in *Dejection*, this state is a mark of belonging:
'and everywhere the blue sky belongs to them, and is their appointed
rest, and their native country and their own natural homes'. But the
situation is also unlike that in *Dejection*, where the opposition of the
luminous and the demonic (on the one hand, the moon, and on the other

* *The Active Universe: Pantheism and the Concept of Imagination in the
English Romantic Poets*, London, 1962, p. 103. Compare also the readings
of Robert Penn Warren (*The Rime of the Ancient Mariner*, New York,
1946) C. M. Bowra (*The Romantic Imagination*, O.U.P., 1950) and James
Benziger (*Images of Eternity*, Carbondale, 1962 p. 26). On the other hand,
proper attention to the demonic theme has been paid by Wilson Knight, in
The Starlit Dome, 1941 ('. . , forgiveness of *reptilian* manifestation remains
basic') and J. B. Beer, in *Coleridge the Visionary*, Chatto, 1959. Mr Beer
has a chapter on 'The Daemonic Sublime' in which he discusses the
ambivalent attitude to the serpent in the mythological literature in which
Coleridge was steeped.

† A liquescent or a silvery moon on the other hand is suggestive in
Lawrence's work of apartness in unison, individuality maintained in the
very self-surrender of love. See *The Rainbow*, p. 49 and p. 124. The 'golden
light' to which Birkin repeatedly refers in 'Moony' serves a comparable
function.

H

the wind making Devil's yule while viper thoughts coil around the mind) is absolute. Here by contrast the demonic is incorporated; moon and water-snakes are embraced in a single vision—atonement entails an acceptance of the viperous. Not that the mariner's salvation is total of course. But the poem itself defines with precision the condition which the mariner himself cannot fully achieve.

Belief in the possibility of a 'paradisal entry into pure, single being'[10] is kept alive throughout *Women in Love* together with a belief that belonging or self-sufficiency or true individuality presupposes communion with death and a re-vitalizing from the fountain of mystic corruption. We are not allowed to rest for long in either belief to the exclusion of the other and perhaps the finest moments are those in which the two beliefs are forced to confront each other and to attest both their antipathy and their affinities.

What it means to be replenished from the mystic source of corruption or disintegration is powerfully suggested in the episode in which Hermione finds Birkin copying a Chinese drawing of geese (in the chapter 'Breadalby').

> 'But why do you copy it?' she asked, casual and sing-song. 'Why not do something original?'
>
> 'I want to know it,' he replied. 'One gets more of China copying this picture, than reading all the books'.
>
> 'And what do you get?'
>
> She was at once roused, she laid as it were violent hands on him, to extract his secrets from him. She must know. It was a dreadful tyranny, an obsession in her, to know all he knew. For some time he was silent, hating to answer her. Then, compelled, he began:
>
> 'I know what centres they live from—what they perceive and feel—the hot, stinging centrality of a goose in the flux of cold water and mud—the curious bitter stinging heat of a goose's blood, entering their own blood like an inoculation of corruptive fire—fire of the cold-burning mud—the lotus mystery.'
>
> Hermione looked at him along her narrow, pallid cheeks. Her eyes were strange and drugged, heavy under their heavy, drooping lids. Her thin bosom shrugged convulsively. He stared back at her, devilish and unchanging. With another strange, sick convulsion, she turned away, as if she were sick, could feel dissolution setting in in her body. For with her mind she was unable to attend to his words; he caught her, as it were, beneath all her defences,

and destroyed her with some insidious occult potency.

'Yes,' she said, as if she did not know what she were saying. 'Yes,' and she swallowed, and tried to regain her mind. But she could not, she was witless, decentralized. Use all her will as she might, she could not recover. She suffered the ghastliness of dissolution, broken and gone in a horrible corruption. And he stood and looked at her unmoved. She strayed out, pallid and preyed-upon like a ghost, like one attacked by the tomb-influences which dog us. And she was gone like a corpse, that has no presence, no connexion. He remained hard and vindictive.

Hermione suffers the ghastliness of dissolution (in the sense of de-composition) because she refuses to dissolve (in the sense of become fluid, yield to the flux). But the actual word dissolve is not used in this second sense. Whereas corruption is assigned a plural value explicitly—corruptive, corruption—the word dissolution occurs only once and the burden of paradox or ironical counterpointing is sustained by a synonym, 'flux'. The Chinese artist lives from a centre as the geese do, sustained by the world of water and mud. The fire flows into the goose's blood and in turn flows into the blood of the artist: barriers are dissolved. So there is connexion, flux and centrality as opposed to isolation and corpse-like dissolution. Hermione battles to maintain her false integrity and pays for it with a squalid subjection to dissolution and corruption. This corruption is the mark of her inability to comprehend the corruptive-fire, the lotus-mystery. We may compare a later passage concerning Mr Crich:

She could see the grey, awful semi-consciousness of mere pain and dissolution coming over him again. . . . Day by day the tissue of the sick man was further and further reduced, nearer and nearer the process came, towards the last knot which held the human being in its unity. But this knot was hard and unrelaxed, the will of the dying man never gave way . . . he was integral, complete.

Like Hermione Mr Crich maintains the false integrity of the will and as a consequence is subdued to the dissolution he refuses to accept.

The achievement of integrity, in short, is a matter of rendering justice to the corruptive agencies of nature as well as the paradisal. I have suggested that some of the finest moments of the novel are those in which tribute is paid at one and the same time to both these agencies. A case in point is the episode at Willey Pond, at the beginning of the chapter 'Moony'.

This episode is the most celebrated in the novel; yet it seems to

have been widely misread, to judge from available commentaries.*
Critics appear to be unanimous that what the scene is centrally about is
Birkin's hatred of the Magna Mater, the accursed Syria Dea; in hurling
stones at the image of the moon he is reacting in fury against female
arrogance—or tyranny, or possessiveness. But the whole incident has
much more to do with integration and disintegration, the need to smash
the false integrity of the ego in order to make possible the true integrity
of the blood.

To understand the scene we need to attend carefully to what immediately precedes it. After Birkin's departure for France Ursula drifts
into a spiritual condition that puts the reader in mind of Gudrun (and
incidentally of Gerald); it is one of those moments in the story when the
sisters seem to have a good deal in common.

> Ursula, left alone, felt as if everything were lapsing out.
> There seemed to be no hope in the world. One was a tiny
> little rock with the tide of nothingness rising higher and
> higher. She herself was real, and only herself—just like
> a rock in a wash of flood-water. The rest was all nothingness.
> She was hard and indifferent, isolated in herself.
>
> There was nothing for it now, but contemptuous,
> resistant indifference. All the world was lapsing into a
> grey wish-wash of nothingness, she had no contact and
> no connexion anywhere.

We recall particularly the Gudrun of 'Coal-Dust', 'cold and separate',
'quite hard and cold and indifferent'. Altogether the passage prepares us
very fully for the assimilation later of woman to moon: compare 'hard
and indifferent' here and, further on, 'She wanted another night, not
this moon-brilliant hardness'. And the early references to brightness and
radiance serve the same purpose:

> She thought she loved, she thought she was full of love.
> This was her idea of herself. But the strange brightness
> of her presence, a marvellous radiance of intrinsic vitality,

* Since I wrote this Mark Kinhead-Weekes has published the essay
to which I have several times had occasion to refer. It is evident that my
own reading of the episode at the Pond is exactly his. However, I have
retained the pages that follow because they are crucial to my argument
and because in any case my analysis goes into more detail than seems to
have suited his particular purposes. But his is the only commentary I
know of in which the essential point is made that the scene illustrates 'the
whole process of recreation through disintegration, infinite going-apart,
that is central to *Women in Love*'. (*Ibid*, pp. 410–12.)

was a luminousness of supreme repudiation, nothing but
repudiation.

So we are very ready to take the significance of the moon when it appears
'with its white and deathly smile': at one level at any rate this is woman
in a 'state of constant unfailing repudiation'—hard, indifferent, dis-
connected. And it is not only Birkin who is repelled. Ursula hurries on
'cowering from the white planet', and when she sees its image in the
water 'for some reason she disliked it'. The moon is herself, but not a self
she is pleased to recognize.

But Ursula's recoil from human society to some extent engages our
sympathy also.

> She loved the horses and cows in the field. Each was
> single and to itself, magical. It was not referred away to
> some detestable social principle. . . . Among the trees, far
> from any human beings, there was a sort of magic peace.
> The more one could find a pure loneliness, with no taint
> of people, the better one felt. She was in reality terrified,
> horrified in her apprehension of people.

Pure loneliness in these early paragraphs is made to seem both desirable
and not desirable. To be separate and yet not coldly isolated, to be
connected with another or others and yet retain one's singleness, to
know specious individuality from true—these are the problems with
which the chapter is centrally concerned.

Ursula, then, longs for true singleness but at this point seems only
capable of isolation. Although she reflects that the animals 'were single
and unsocial as she herself was' their magical singleness is in fact something she aspires towards rather than something she has achieved. So the
significance of Birkin's stone-throwing would appear to be clear: it is an
attack on that deathly supremacy of the ego that makes for mere
separateness and indifference. 'And I wouldn't give a straw for your
female ego—it's a rag doll', he says angrily in the discussion that follows.
His violence renews the flow of life, which is at the same time a flowing
in of darkness. The pure supremacy of light—the supremacy of the ego—
gives way to a proper tension between light and dark: 'Darts of bright
light shot asunder, darkness swept over the centre.' Emblematically
Birkin's stoning of the moon brings about that singleness of being which
later in the chapter he recognizes as the main object of his quest:

> . . . a lovely state of free proud singleness, which accepted
> the obligation of the permanent connexion with others,

and with the other, submits to the yoke and leash of love,
but never forfeits its own proud individual singleness, even
while it loves and yields.

The image of the moon yields before the aggressive male yet never
forfeits its singleness. 'It was reasserting itself, the inviolable moon'; the
ebbing flakes of light 'were gathering a heart again, they were coming
once more into being'; 'a distorted, frayed moon was shaking upon the
waters again, reasserted, renewed, trying to recover from its convulsion,
to get over the disfigurement and the agitation, to be whole and com-
posed, at peace'. The individuality of the ego gives way to a true individuality, though a precarious one.

There is a passage in the essay *Love* which lends some support to
this interpretation:

> But the love between a man and a woman, when it is
> whole, is dual. It is the melting into pure communion, and
> it is the friction of sheer sensuality, both.
> . . . There must be two in one, always two in one—the
> sweet love of communion and the fierce, proud love of
> sensual fulfilment, both together in one love. And then
> we are like a rose. We surpass even love, love is en-
> compassed and surpassed. We are two who have a pure
> connexion. We are two, isolated like gems in our unthink-
> able otherness. But the rose contains and transcends us,
> we are one rose, beyond.[11]

In 'Moony' also the rose is used as an image of the right kind of singleness:

> . . . He saw the moon regathering itself insidiously, saw the
> heart of the rose intertwining vigorously and blindly . . .
> until a ragged rose, a distorted, frayed moon was shaking
> upon the waters again . . .

The comparison of novel and essay is valid I think, even though in the
essay hard brilliance is the mark of a wholly *legitimate* otherness, as it is
not in the novel.

In case I appear to be labouring the obvious in this exegesis, I had
better point out again that though commentators have agreed in admiring
the episode at the Pond wholeheartedly they have had nothing to say
about what seems to me its central meaning. Their attention has all been
given to a theme that is subsidiary to the one I have been discussing; they
have been hypnotized by Birkin's reference to Cybele, 'the accursed
Syria Dea'. Middleton Murry began it all by claiming that:

Birkin is destroying Aphrodite, the divinity under whose cold light Ursula annihilated the core of intrinsic male in Lawrence's last incarnation as Anton Skrebensky. To annihilate the female insatiably demanding physical satisfaction from the man who cannot give it to her—the female who has thus annihilated him—this is Lawrence's desire.[12]

And if we turn from Murry to Leavis we find a comment which, stripped of much that is unacceptable in Murry's, and buttressed with qualifications, is, for all that, no more useful in the end. We are still left with the impression that the episode is predominantly about female posesssiveness.

In Ursula, Birkin finds something to be fought before the hope of a permanent relation can be assured—something he calls the 'Magna Mater' . . . The possessiveness he divines in Ursula is what (though that, we may feel, is not all) he sees in the reflected moon . . .[13] (etc.)

And here is Graham Hough on the 'second layer of significance' in this 'famous scene':

. . . it is clear enough that the moon is the white goddess, the primal woman image, *das ewig weibliche*, by whom he is obviously haunted. He tries to drive her away, but of course she always comes back; as soon as he stops his stone-throwing the moon-image re-forms.[14]

True, Birkin has attacked the image of the Great Mother quite openly earlier in the novel, with reference to the arrogant pretensions of Ursula and Hermione, and no one would want to deny that the invocation of Cybele links that passage and this. But here the theme of female tyranny is strictly subordinate to the theme of female isolation (that impulse to separateness that Lawrence called elsewhere—in *England, My England*—'the cold white light of feminine independence'). Yet this interpretation also needs to be qualified, for in the last analysis the episode is concerned with human isolation as such, of which feminine isolation is but the type. (And this certainly is what one might expect if one were to come to the novel direct from *Fantasia of the Unconscious*: 'The moon is the centre of our terrestrial individuality in the cosmos. . . . She it is who burns white with the intense friction of her withdrawal into separation, that cold, proud white fire of furious, almost malignant apartness, the struggle into fierce, frictional separation.') If Birkin's reference to Cybele were excised the episode would not lose greatly in point or in power; as parable it would remain intact, a dramatic rendering of the disintegration of the isolate female ego, and the precarious achievement of true single-ness.*

But I want to devote a little more space to substantiating this reading. In his heated exchanges later with Ursula, Birkin declares:

> 'I want you to drop your assertive *will*, your frightened apprehensive self-insistence, that is what I want.'

This makes explicit a meaning that has hitherto been implicit. The radiance of the moon is inescapable, just as Ursula's suffering is, or her 'state of constant unfailing repudiation'. And it is strongly implied that

* Leavis and Hough it will be observed, take it for granted that the shattered image of the moon returns to its original state: 'It does, of course, re-form finally'; 'as soon as he stops his stone-throwing the moon-image re-forms'. But if we consult the text this is what we find:

> . . . until a ragged rose, a distorted, frayed moon was shaking upon the waters again, reasserted, renewed, trying to recover from its convulsion, to get over the disfigurement and agitation, to be whole and composed, at peace.

No doubt we are aware with a part of our minds that the moon-image must eventually return to the static condition it was in prior to the stoning, but Lawrence's art contrives to prevent this knowledge from asserting itself as relevant. If his art did not do so the scene would indeed spell 'ineluctable defeat' for Birkin. Leavis denies that in fact it does spell defeat; but he points to nothing that can be taken to be positive evidence for the truth of this assertion. More recently Murray Krieger, subscribing to much the same reading as Hough and Leavis, spells out even more clearly the assumption that the return of the moon to its previous static state is part of the given meaning; indeed for him it is central to the meaning.

> . . . 'It was re-asserting itself, the inviolable moon'. And inevitably it is to the unbroken calm, to what Gide called 'the terrifying fixity . . . the immobility of death' that the moon returns.

As evidence for this assertion he proceeds to quote the passage I have myself quoted in this note. His chapter ends like this:

> As we witness Ursula's desire to monopolise Rupert, we are meant to wonder if one is ever totally free from the clutches of the Magna Mater. After all, at the crucial symbolic moment, Birkin, for all the fury of his stoning, could not keep the face of the moon from inevitably reasserting itself on the still surface of the pond.[15]

This is merely the normal reading carried to an extreme.

if she constantly suffers it is because of the constant presence and asser-tiveness of her own self: 'the strange brightness of her presence'; 'She herself was real, and only herself'. And this self-insistence or radiant assertiveness, which is at once 'triumphant' and 'apprehensive', goes with an unfailing self-awareness. Ursula is oppressed with a sense that the moon is constantly watching her—in other words that she is being constantly watched by her own self. So when she overhears Birkin soliloquizing it is significant that his first words should be 'You can't go away . . . There *is* no away. You only withdraw upon yourself'.

A useful gloss on this aspect of the meaning is Lawrence's review of Trigant Burrow's book *The Social Basis of Consciousness*.

> . . . And gradually Dr. Burrow realized that to fit life every time to a theory is in itself a mechanistic process, a process of unconscious repression, a process of image-substitution.
> . . . The analyst wants to break all this image business, so that life can flow freely. But it is useless to try to do so by replacing in the unconscious another image—this time, the image, the fixed motive of the incest-complex.
> . . . If, then, Dr. Burrow asks himself, it is not sex-repression which is at the root of the neurosis of modern life, what is it?
> . . . The real trouble lies in the inward sense of "separate-ness" which dominates every man. At a certain point in his evolution, man became cognitively conscious: he bit the apple: he began to know. Up till that time his con-sciousness flowed unaware, as in the animals. Suddenly, his consciousness split.
> . . . Perhaps the most interesting part of Dr. Burrow's book is his examination of normality. As soon as man became aware of himself, he made a picture of himself. Then he began to live according to the picture. Mankind at large made a picture of itself, and every man had to conform to the picture: the ideal.
> . . . The true self is not aware that it is a self. A bird as it sings, sings itself. But not according to a picture. It has no idea of itself.
> And this is what the analyst must try to do: to liberate his patient from his own image, from his horror of his own isolation and the horror of the 'stoppage' of his real vital flow.
> . . . Men must get back into *touch*. And to do so they must forfeit the vanity and the *noli me tangere* of their own

absoluteness: also they must utterly break the present great picture of a normal humanity: shatter that mirror in which we all live grimacing: and fall again into true relatedness.[16]

'Break all this image business, so that life can flow freely'; 'shatter that mirror': the relevance of this to the episode in 'Moony' is surely clear.* And compare 'your own image ... your *idea* of yourself' (from the review) with 'This was her idea of herself'; or 'the horror of his own isolation' with 'isolated in herself'; or 'social, or image consciousness' with 'referred away to some detestable social principle'—and so on. When allowances have been made for the difference between fictional and non-fictional modes of writing we can fairly claim that what is said in the review is also said in 'Moony'. 'The true self is not aware that it is a self', is not divided: image consciousness is the enemy of true singleness.

The reading I have so far proposed is borne out, I believe, by what occurs in the remainder of the chapter. I have already dealt at sufficient length with Birkin's reflections on the African statuette, but I should at least remark here that these reflections are concerned with nothing if not with the achievement of pure single being in the teeth of forces that make for disintegration and dissolution. If 'the moon is the white goddess, the primal woman image' and only or even primarily that, then Birkin's thoughts here have very little bearing on the episode by the pond, which immediately precedes them and which they seem in intention at any rate to grow out of.

And in fact they do grow out of that episode, though not altogether directly. First there is an assertion of the need to dissolve and then (as always) a counter-assertion of the need to resist dissolution, an exposure of the monstrous threat to the soul's integrity that lies precisely in dissolution, disintegration and darkness. But the counter-assertion is already implicit in the moon-stoning scene itself; that is why we pass so easily to the discursive passage that follows, even though in the parable of the moon and how it yielded up its separateness before the influx of darkness the *word* dissolution is never used, and even though the African

---

* Earlier in the novel, in the chapter 'Class-Room', the metaphor of the mirror is used with full deliberation:

'It's all that Lady of Shalott business', he said, in his strong abstract voice. He seemed to be charging her before the unseeing air. 'You've got that mirror, your own fixed will, your immortal understanding, your own tight conscious world, and there is nothing beyond, it. There, in the mirror, you must have everything. . . .'

dissolution is, at the most obvious level, sinister, as the darkness with which the moon's image contends is not.

I pass now to the abortive proposal and its aftermath. Not that the next episode, the encounter with Brangwen, is a mere irrelevance:

> What Brangwen thought himself to be, how meaningless it was, confronted with the reality of him. Birkin could see only a strange, inexplicable, almost patternless collection of passions and desires and suppressions and traditions and mechanical ideas, all cast unfused and disunited into this slender, bright-faced man of nearly fifty, who was as unresolved now as he was at twenty, and as uncreated.

We find even here the concern with integrity and image-consciousness. But with the entry of Ursula this theme dominates once more; in particular, the metaphors of light and radiance again become frequent and insist on the relevance of this latter part of the chapter to the scene at Willey Pond.

> Her face was bright and abstracted as usual, with the abstraction, that look of being not quite *there*, not quite present to the facts of reality, that galled her father so much.

Her father's violent attack on her is a kind of parody of Birkin's assault on the image of the moon; a parody, for Birkin's violence imposed itself on the reader as legitimate and necessary, whereas Brangwen's clearly is mere bullying. Its immediate effect is to drive his daughter back into her bright hard isolation.

> Ursula's face closed, she completed herself against them all. Recoiling upon herself, she became hard and self-completed, like a jewel. . . . She was so radiant with all things in her possession of perfect hostility.

In this condition she gangs up with Gudrun against the whole male sex:

> Only Gudrun was in accord with her. It was at these times that the intimacy between the two sisters was most complete, as if their intelligence were one. They felt a strong, bright bond of understanding between them, surpassing everything else. And during all these days of blind bright abstraction and intimacy of his two daughters, the father seemed to breathe an air of death, as if he were destroyed in his very being. . . . They continued radiant in their easy female transcendency.

(This looks back to 'The moon was transcendent over the bare, open space, she suffered from being exposed to it.') Gudrun is unable to distinguish between the two kinds of male violence, Birkin's and Brangwen's, and she discusses the one as though it were the other. Of Birkin she says: 'He cries you down . . . And by mere force of violence.' Soon enough however Ursula reacts against Gudrun, whom she begins to suspect of an 'irreverence, destructive of all true life'. Yet we are not left at the end of the chapter with an Ursula who has been won over to Birkin's point of view.

> She was not at all sure that it was this mutual unison in separateness that she wanted. She wanted unspeakable intimacies. She wanted to have him, utterly, finally to have him as her own, oh, so unspeakably, in intimacy.

This reminds us of her relationship with Gudrun:

> They exchanged confidences, they were intimate in their revelations to the last degree, giving each other at last every secret. They withheld nothing, they told everything, till they were over the border of evil.

(Compare 'the intimacy between the two sisters' and 'during all these days of blind *bright* abstraction and intimacy of his two daughters'.) Though she is not radically corrupt as Gudrun is, Ursula too, with her mistaken ideal of pure love and her mistaken desire for intimacy, works against true singleness.

In short, the theme enunciated at the beginning of the chapter is dominant to the end.

> She believed that love far surpassed the individual. He said the individual was more than love, or than any relationship. For him, the bright, single soul accepted love as one of its conditions, a condition of its own equilibrium. She believed that love was *everything*.

It has been made clear throughout the chapter that there are *kinds* of separateness and *kinds* of brightness, so that the significance of 'bright, single soul' inevitably registers itself as complex. The phrase recognizes for the last time the positive virtue in brightness or the impulse towards separateness, reminding us that this impulse, which may make for indifference and isolation, is precisely that which makes for true singleness or integrity. And this is characteristic of a novel in which the sources of life are so deeply and variously implicated with the sources of death.

Our sense that in the account of Birkin's stoning of the moon's image a great deal of the significance of the novel has been concentrated in a rich and satisfying emblem is thoroughly justified. What we particularly note is the perfect justice done to the activities of departure *and* coming together, breaking down *and* creation. The more violent Birkin becomes the more the flakes of light struggle to achieve a paradisal serenity and unity; and neither is triumphant.

> And departure is the opposite equivalent of coming together; decay, corruption, destruction, breaking down is the opposite equivalent of creation.[17]

It may be granted that Birkin's violence has no immediate and obvious relevance to the activity of *decay* or *corruption*; and yet, intricately and variously, the language refers us back to numerous occasions where we have registered human or non-human activity as lethal and corruptive. 'Burst', 'exploded', 'white and dangerous fire', 'incandescent', 'not yet violated', 'violent pangs', 'white-burning', 'tormented', 'convulsive': one thinks how closely this vocabulary has been associated with Gerald and Gudrun; it is partly in these terms, that Birkin defined for Ursula that 'inverse process' of 'destructive creation' in which (at this moment in history—'at the end of a great era or epoch') we all of us in some degree find ourselves involved. This is that rhetoric of disruption that Lawrence uses for his most equivocal purposes—a marvellously sensitive medium for suggesting, among other things, a quality of dangerous, non-organic vitality.

Indeed, given this violence of Birkin's at the Pond, we need not be surprised to find that his explicit repudiation of the awful African process does not in the event represent the whole truth about him. If earlier, at Breadalby, he had annihilated Hermione with 'corruptive fire—fire of the cold-burning mud', he destroys the false individuality of Ursula now with an energy which, again, is burning and disruptive— distinguishable from the African sun-destruction and yet analogous to it. So the fragments of the moon, 'falling back as in panic, but working their way home again persistently', image a process at once reductive and integrative, violent and peace-loving, demonic and paradisal. In effect, two traditions of Romanticism—two concepts of belonging, or ideals of self-sufficiency—are compelled to confront each other here, and indeed in the novel at large; and in the confrontation neither is affirmed at the expense of the other. It is in this spirit of course that Birkin postulates the incorporating of the heavenly *and* hellish:

'. . . he says he believes that a man and wife can go further than any other two beings—but *where*, is not explained. They can know each other, heavenly and hellish, but particularly hellish, so perfectly that they go beyond heaven and hell—into—there it all breaks down—into nowhere.'

'Into Paradise, he says,' laughed Gerald.

Gudrun's scepticism is repellent, certainly; but there is a sense also in which it is endorsed, raising as it does the disconcerting question whether any human being could actually achieve such disparate ends, so rich an inclusiveness. In fact what the novel as a whole tends to suggest (I take up this topic again later) is that the kind of fulfilment or completeness that Birkin aspires to is both necessary and impossible.

IV Savage Visionaries

The paradisal entry into pure, single being is proposed by Birkin momentarily as the way of redemption; yet we are aware in *Women in Love* as a whole of a complexity of issues to which this solution seems scarcely adequate. And indeed (as already noted) Birkin's conclusions are not finally endorsed—in any simple way at any rate; justice is done also to darker compulsions, and the novel's richness and achieved poise is the consequence. Yet if Lawrence makes no surrender to the paradisal myth in *Women in Love*, he can certainly be said to have done so in other work, in the sense that, postulating over-simple solutions, he occasionally denies his own 'principle of decomposition', denies in other words his own most genuine perceptions. *Lady Chatterley's Lover* is a case in point, and also *The Ladybird*. I consider both of these works later, using as foils both *Women in Love* and a tale that seems to me conspicuously successful, *England, My England*.

With the wisdom of hindsight we can perhaps detect even in his earliest work how Lawrence might indulge in paradisal evasions, proposing solutions more simple in fact than they have the air of being or, given the complexity of the issues raised in the story, need to be. There is an instance in *The White Peacock*. In the chapter 'The Scent of Blood' we learn that before the death of her father Lettie 'had sought the bright notes in everything'.

> Lately, however, she had noticed again the cruel pitiful crying of a hedgehog caught in a gin, and she had noticed the traps for the fierce little murderers, traps walled in with a small fence of fir, and baited with the guts of a killed rabbit.

Leslie endeavours to conduct the courtship entirely on the pastoral-sentimental level, an approach that Lettie from time to time rebels against. During the course of a day spent at the farm she goes with Cyril and Emily to the 'bottom pond, a pool chained in heavy growth of weeds. It was moving with rats, the father had said'. This lower pond received the overflow from the upper pond 'by a turmoil from the deep black sluice'. They watched the rats in the water.

> One dropped with an ugly plop into the water, and swam towards us, the hoary imp, his sharp snout and his wicked little eyes moving at us. Lettie shuddered. I threw a stone into the dead pool, and frightened them all. But we had frightened ourselves more, so we hurried away, and stamped our feet in relief on the free pavement of the yard.

Later the three of them are joined by Leslie and George, and together they all watch the rising of the moon. Leslie wants to utter his half-finished proposal but Lettie, fearful of being caught in the toils of sentiment, breaks free and begins to dance. The night and the moon spin 'a little madness' and finally she becomes exhilarated like a Bacchante.

The demonic energy which Lettie releases, and which the decorous and sentimental Leslie feels to be such an affront to his own tender mood, is something positive and admirable. But our sense of this is qualified by our sense too of the ferocity and malevolence which the free play of natural energies may easily entail: the ferocity of the murderous hedgehogs and the ugly malevolence of the water-rats. Intimations of cruelty in nature are overlaid with more disturbing intimations of obscenity and repulsiveness.* But whether the cruelty or the repulsiveness is the more relevant to this particular human story is left undetermined. This is not in itself a flaw of course. For though Lettie surrenders to wild impulse in this particular episode, the surrender has

---

* It is perhaps worth remarking how traditionally Romantic the imagery in this chapter is. The hedgehogs and the water-rats belong with Coleridge's water-snakes. Whether one denies the demonic with the oblivious insensitivity of the mariner or from timidity, idealism and snobbery, as Leslie does, the result is the same: isolation and the resurgence of the demonic in visions of animal corruption and malevolence. The victim here however is not in the end Leslie himself but George, the scapegoat, who dies effectively in the body long before his actual death, and ends in a pathetic stupor of estrangement:

> We were all uncomfortably impressed with the sense of our alienation from him. He sat apart and obscure among us, like a condemned man.

no consequences. It is not as though the story were concerned to work out very seriously the implications of 'letting go', as *Women in Love* and some of the *Tales* are. On the contrary, it is the fate of Lettie and Leslie *not* to let go.

But where the theme of self-destruction, or self-abandon, *is* Lawrence's central concern he cannot afford to be as indecisive as he is in *The White Peacock*. Hence, I think, the comparative failure of *The Ladybird*. Early in this story Count Dionys tells Lady Daphne that he has 'found the God who pulls things down . . . not the devil of destruction, but the god of destruction. The blessed god of destruction . . . The god of anger, who throws down the steeples and the factory chimneys'. We remember this when later on, during the Count's visit to Voynich Hall, the significance of his strange emblem, the Mary-beetle, comes up for discussion.

> 'The scarab *is* a piquant insect,' said Basil.
>
> 'Do you know Fabre?' put in Lord Beveridge. 'He suggests that the beetle rolling a little ball of dung before him, in a dry old field, must have suggested to the Egyptians the First Principle that set the globe rolling. And so the scarab became the symbol of the creative principle—or something like that.'
>
> 'That the earth is a tiny ball of dry dung is good,' said Basil.
>
> 'Between the claws of a ladybird,' added Daphne.
>
> 'That is what it is, to go back to one's origin,' said Lady Beveridge.
>
> 'Perhaps they meant that it was the principle of decomposition which first set the ball rolling,' said the Count.
>
> 'The ball would have to be *there* first,' said Basil.
>
> 'Certainly. But it hadn't started to roll. Then the principle of decomposition started it.' The Count smiled as if it were a joke.
>
> 'I am no Egyptologist,' said Lady Beveridge, 'so I can't judge.'

We seem to have here a variant on the principle of positive destruction that we have already heard about; like destruction, decomposition can be creative. Moreover, given the title of the story, we have a right to suppose that this exchange of ideas about the scarab is of special thematic significance and will throw light upon the events that follow. In fact it does nothing of the sort and instead of a fable about destruction and decomposition we get the story as it stands:

> No, she had found this wonderful thing after she had
> heard him singing: she had suddenly collapsed away
> from her old self into this darkness, this peace, this
> quiescence that was like a full dark river flowing eternally
> in her soul. She had gone to sleep from the *nuit blanche* of
> her days.

This full dark river is a river of dissolution, but not dissolution in the
sense of decomposition. The story has simply turned its back on the
implied proposition that there is an essential regenerative value in
corruption.

The fact that Lawrence is prepared to use the scarab here as an
image of creative destruction, or lively decomposition, provides in its
way indirect confirmation of my argument that the passage about the
scarab in *Women in Love* ought not to be taken merely at its face value.

> This was why her face looked like a beetle's: this was why
> the Egyptians worshipped the ball-rolling scarab: because
> of the principle of knowledge in dissolution and corruption.

In the context of the novel as a whole, that negative statement (I have
argued) is considerably qualified, and we ought not to be surprised to
find that Egyptian values are later emphatically endorsed:

> He sat still like an Egyptian Pharoah, driving the car. He
> felt as if he were seated in immemorial potency, like the
> great carven statues of real Egypt . . . A lambent intelligence
> played secondarily above his pure Egyptian concentration
> in darkness. . . . He would be night-free, like an Egyptian.

Dionys also has his moment of identification with an Egyptian King-
God, but whereas the novel faces up honestly to everything implied by
this identification (corruption, degradation, a descent into the slime) the
tale does not; here we can comfortably forget that there is a great danger
involved in invoking the god of destruction, or decomposition. The
scarab—roughly analogous in evocative value to the water-rats in *The
White Peacock*—makes its appearance only to be forgotten; or if it isn't
altogether forgotten might just as well be. The song that so hypnotizes
Lady Daphne in the night is about a swan that loves a hunter, and turns
into a woman so as to marry him. Finally she leaves him and her
children and becomes a swan again. The metamorphosis reminds us
that there is another ladybird in the story, 'the beetle rolling a little ball
of dung before him, in a dry old field'! But what are we to make of this
association of dung and glamour, once we recognize it? If a transvalua-

tion of the one into the other is intended (but there is very little to support the supposition) nothing is done linguistically to effect it.

In the essay *Art and Morality* Lawrence remarked:

> Design, in art, is a recognition of the relation between various things, various elements in the creative flux. You can't *invent* a design. You recognize it, in the fourth dimension. That is, with your blood and your bones, as well as with your eyes.
>
> Egypt had a wonderful relation to a vast living universe, only dimly visual in its reality. The dim eye-vision and the powerful blood-feeling of the Negro African, even today, gives us strange images, which our eyes can hardly see, but which we know are surpassing. The big silent statue of Rameses is like a drop of water, hanging through the centuries in dark suspense, and never static. The African fetish-statues have no movement, visually represented. Yet one little motionless wooden figure stirs more than all the Parthenon frieze. It sits in the place where no Kodak can snap it.*

We recall how it is said of Lady Daphne:

> She never *saw* him, as a lover. When she saw him, he was the little officer, a prisoner, quiet, claiming nothing in all the world. And when she went to him as his lover, his wife, it was always dark.

We might define the flaw in *The Ladybird* by observing that it turns out to be a story about 'Egypt' in one of its senses only—'dim eye-vision and . . . powerful blood feeling'—though it had made claims at one point to a more inclusive concern, one which would embrace also the Egyptian principle of decomposition.

> . . . she had suddenly collapsed away from her old self into this darkness, this peace, this quiescence that was like a full dark river flowing eternally in her soul.

In a story dedicated to the god of destruction this soothing resolution can only affect us as an evasion.

---

* In the light of this passage a reading of *Women in Love* that discovers a positive as well as negative value in the fetishes becomes just that more persuasive.

There are no such evasions in *England, My England*. This tale first appeared in October 1915 (in the *English Review*) and we notice that some of the dominant imagery of another work published in the latter part of that year, *The Crown*, is exploited here too:

> Strange how the savage England lingers in patches: as here, amid these shaggy gorse commons, and marshy, snake-infested places near the foot of the south downs.

Leavis remarks that the story has for its theme 'a man who refuses responsibility'. True; but much more than this, Egbert is a man whose refusal of responsibility is at the same time a refusal to acknowledge the great principle of corruption, which is also the principle of power. There is a passage in *The Crown* which is virtually identical with one in the tale.

> One day there was a loud, terrible scream from the garden, tearing the soul. Oh, and it was a snake lying on the warm garden bed, and in his teeth the leg of a frog, a frog spread out, screaming with horror.

And so in the story:

> One day Winifred heard the strangest scream from the flower-bed under the low window of the living room . . .

In the essay Lawrence goes on to comment:

> We were all white with fear. But why? In the world of twilight as in the world of light, one beast shall devour another. The world of corruption has its stages, where the lower shall devour the higher, *ad infinitum*.

This serves as a pointer (supposing it were needed) to what is central in the story: Egbert's inability to recognize, until personal tragedy teaches him, that ours is a twilit world of corruption as well as a world of light. He and his young wife achieve in the early days of their marriage the kind of satisfaction which is popularly supposed to sum up Lawrence's notions of fulfilment.

> Ah, that it might never end, this passion, this marriage! The flame of their two bodies burnt again into that old cottage, that was haunted already by so much bygone physical desire. You could not be in the dark room for an hour without the influences coming over you. The hot blood-desire of bygone yeomen, there in this old den where they had lusted and bred for so many generations. The silent house, dark, with thick, timbered walls and the big black chimney-place, and the sense of secrecy.

But what is not incorporated into their living is the truth—or values—represented by the snake-infested marsh.

> There is a natural marsh in my belly, and there the snake
> is naturally at home . . .

So Lawrence was to affirm in *The Reality of Peace*, and the burden of that essay is that if the snake is not acknowledged he will declare himself with a peculiar, foul virulence. And so it is with Egbert, who begins now to be identified with the principle he has denied.

> His heart went back to the savage old spirit of the place:
> the desire for old gods, lost passions, the passion of the
> cold-blooded, darting snakes that hissed and shot away
> from him, the mystery of blood-sacrifices, all the lost,
> intense sensations of the primeval people of the place,
> whose passions seethed in the air still, from those long
> days before the Romans came. The seethe of a lost,
> dark passion in the air. The presence of unseen snakes.

And not only does Egbert himself become snake-like ('As soon as sympathy, like a soft hand, was reached out to touch him, away he swerved, instinctively, as a harmless snake swerves and swerves and swerves away from the outstretched hand') but so does his crippled child. They both of them 'flicker' in a way that reminds us irresistibly of the snake: 'that flickering, wicked little smile that seemed to haunt his face'; 'the child flickered back to him with an answering smile of irony and recklessness.'

And yet we cannot but acknowledge that the new self released in each of them is attractive as well as repellent.* Better, in one sense, the sardonic Egbert than the 'born rose' adored by his infant children.

> But of the complete failure of [Egbert's] life we are left
> in no doubt (and we are left in no doubt of the essential
> moral).

* There is point here in recalling some remarks about Pearl in the essay on Hawthorne (I quote from the uncollected version):

> Pearl by the very openness of her perversity, was at least
> straightforward. She answers downright that she has no
> Heavenly Father. She mocks and tortures Dimmesdale with
> a subtlety rarer even than her mother's, and more exquisitely
> poisonous. But even in this she has a sort of reckless
> gallantry, the pride of her own deadly being. We cannot
> help regarding the phenomenon of Pearl with wonder, and
> fear, and amazement, and respect. For surely nowhere in
> literature is the spirit of much of modern childhood so
> profoundly, almost magically revealed.

So Leavis comments;[2] but the comment seems to me of very doubtful value. For surely Egbert is no such unqualified failure. The word 'moral' here is especially unfortunate. Indeed we might well compare Egbert with the wickedly and attractively sardonic Birkin:

> Birkin was dancing with Ursula. There were odd little fires playing in his eyes, he seemed to have turned into something wicked and flickering, mocking, suggestive, quite impossible. Ursula was frightened of him, and fascinated.

Wicked, flickering, mocking: it is the spirit of the later Egbert. We might even lay the words 'black magic', from *Women in Love* ('carried her through the air as if without strength, through black magic') next to 'old dark magic of parental authority' or 'forbidden secret society', a phrase used of the bond between the father and the crippled child. And as Ursula becomes acquainted with degradation ('What was degrading? Who cared?') so does Egbert:

> An ugly little look came on to his face, of a man who has accepted his own degradation.

There is a crucial difference of course. Egbert, having failed to acknowledge degradation, is now subdued to it—by the kind of law we observe to be operative in the life of Hermione. Yet as Hermione, dissolved and corrupted by her own black hatred of Birkin, communicates momentarily with a dark reality from which her egoism normally cuts her off, so Egbert in the last phase of his life is borne along the potent river of dissolution; and his final surrender to it is at once a defeat and a victory.

> Better the agony of dissolution ahead than the nausea of the effort backwards. Better the terrible work should go forward, the dissolving into the black sea of death, in the extremity of dissolution, than that there should be any reaching back towards life. To forget! To forget! Utterly, utterly to forget, in the great forgetting of death.

'Better the terrible work should go forward'. One thinks of Ursula:

> She could feel, within the darkness, the terrible assertion of the body, the unutterable anguish of dissolution. . . .
> But better die than live mechanically a life that is a repetition of repetitions. To die is to move on with the invisible.'

In the course of Ursula's reflections the self-destructiveness that is an anguished but liberating surrender of the will ('She yielded, she gave up') is defined and evaluated through a simple *contrast* with the obscene and brutalizing destructiveness of war:

> . . . and there was no escape, save in death.
> But what a joy! What a gladness to think that whatever humanity did, it could not seize hold of the kingdom of death, to nullify that. The sea they turned into a murderous alley and a soiled road of commerce, disputed like the dirty land of a city every inch of it. The air they claimed too, shared it up, parcelled it out to certain owners, they trespassed in the air to fight for it . . .
> But the great dark, illimitable kingdom of death, there humanity was put to scorn.

In the tale however it is not as easy as this to distinguish between the two kinds of destructiveness; and indeed the effect is a good deal more subtle than in the novel.

> Let the black sea of death itself solve the problem of futurity. Let the will of man break and give up.

Where does self-murder end and true self-destructiveness begin?

England, My England first appeared, as I have said, in October 1915. How mixed Lawrence's feelings were about the current war, in its early stages, and how those feelings get into the language at the end of this tale is apparent if we consider the following passage from the *Study of Thomas Hardy*, which was apparently written in the months August-November 1914:

> Does not the war show us how little, under all our careful-ness, we count human life and human suffering, how little we value ourselves at bottom, how we hate our own security?
> . . . It is no war for the freedom of man from militarism or the Prussian yoke; it is a war for freedom of the bonds of our own cowardice and sluggish greed of security and well-being; it is a fight to regain ourselves out of the grip of our own caution.
> Tell me no more we care about human life and suffering. We are, every one of us, revelling at this moment in the squandering of human life as if it were something we needed. And it is shameful. And all because that, to *live*, we are afraid to risk ourselves. We can only die.[3]

Manifestly, support may be found here for a reading of *England, My England* that pays full regard to the positive-negative value of Egbert's submission to dissolution.

It is characteristic of Lawrence that this dissolution, the culmination of a slow regressive and *downward* movement, should at the same time be a movement *outwards*, a lapsing-out on the great darkness, a dissipating or visionary commingling: the harking back to the old savage spirit of place ends in the obliteration of the isolate self. Again and again in his fiction Lawrence suggests that these two movements are ultimately one. And not only in his fiction; in the first version of the essay on *Herman Melville's* TYPEE *and* OMOO he remarks—

> Melville makes the great return. He would really melt himself, an elemental, back into his vast beloved element, material though it is. All his fire would carry down, quench in the sea. It is time for the sea to receive back her own, into the pale bluish underworld of the watery after-life.

And this re-absorption, or release into infinity, is at the same time a degradation, a return to the savage:*

> Nothing is more startling, at once actual and dream-mystical, than [Melville's] descent *down* the gorges to the valley of the dreadful Typee. *Down* this narrow, steep, horrible dark gorge he slides and struggles as we struggle in a dream, or in the act of birth, to emerge in the green Eden of the first, or last era, the valley of the timeless savages. He had dreaded this entry acutely, for the men of Typee had a cannibal reputation. But they are good and gentle with him, he finds himself at once in a pure, mysterious world, pristine. (*Italics mine.*)

'At once actual and dream-mystical': this note is struck again and again—

> For many thousands of years the Pacific lands have been passing through the process of disturbing dreams, some good, mostly bad, dreams of the great sensual-mystic civilisations which once were theirs, and which are now ten times forgotten by the very people themselves.

* The dual process I am concerned with here is not, after all, essentially different from the process I have already commented on in dealing with the argument of *The Crown* (see above p. 59):

> *Corruption* will at last break down for us the deadened forms, and release us into the *infinity*.

Or:

> But Samoa, Tahiti, Nukuheva are the sleep and the forgetting of this great life, the very body of dreams. To which dream Melville helplessly returns.

Or:

> Melville found in Typee almost what he wanted to find, what every man dreams of finding: a perfect home among timeless, unspoiled savages.

Whether the immediate topic is the culture of Typee or Melville's response to that culture, the emphasis is still on that duality of apprehension which I began by considering: the degradation,* the descent into savagery, is at the same time a heightening of the capacity for dream-perception and for sensual-mystic communication, at-one-ment.

> After all, cannibalism seems everywhere to have primarily a ritualistic, sacramental meaning. It is no doubt the remains of the mystic Eucharist of the sensual religions, the very counter-part of our Eucharist. . . . In Typee they observed the strictest secrecy. There was evidently a real passional comprehension of the sacrament, the mystery of *oneing* which takes place when the communicant partakes of the body of his vanished enemy. It is the mystery of final unification, ultimate oneing, as in our sacrament.

In effect, an equation is established once again between dissolution as degradation and dissolution as fusion; and one thinks of *Women in Love* and the way the African dissolution is assimilated to a dissolution appropriate to the visionary, or seer, or dreamer. Clearly, pitfalls yawn here, in this oblique equation of savage and mystic—possibilities of dishonesty, or sentimentality, or bathos—and it is a measure of Lawrence's achievement in *Women in Love* that he so completely avoids them. By way of enforcing this point I want to consider, along with *Women in Love*, a work that is very evidently a product of the same *Zeitgeist*, Conrad's *Heart of Darkness*—a tale in which one remarks a kind of evasiveness, a flirting with the theme of degradation, that it is the strength of *Women in Love* (and also of *England, My England*) to be free of (though it is not unlike the kind of evasiveness to be found in *The Ladybird*).

---

* The final version of the essay is far more emphatic than this one concerning the savage's degradation:

> But we cannot turn the current of our own life backwards, back towards their soft warm twilight and uncreate mud. Not for a moment. If we do it for a moment, it makes us sick.

The dark river flowing from the heart of Africa, and from the darkness of pre-history, puts us in mind inevitably of Lawrence's river of dissolution. And there is another metaphor—a less obvious one—that is common to both the tale and *Women in Love*, the metaphor of the brink or threshold or limit; the human soul is apt to be conceived of in both works as standing right on the edge of the vast darkness, or perhaps going over, going beyond.

> This is the reason why I affirm that Kurtz was a remarkable man. He had something to say. He said it. Since I had peeped *over the edge* myself, I understand better the meaning of his stare . . .
>
> True he had made that last stride, he had stepped *over the edge* . . . And perhaps in this is the whole difference; perhaps all the wisdom, all the truth, and all sincerity, are just compressed into that inappreciable moment of time in which we step *over the threshold* of the invisible.
>
> . . . the whisper of a voice speaking from *beyond the threshold* of an eternal darkness.
>
> . . . this alone had beguiled his unlawful soul *beyond the bounds* of permitted aspirations.

The title of the chapter that gives an account of Mr Crich's slow dissolution towards death is 'Threshold'. It is said of Ursula and Gudrun that

> They withheld nothing, they told everything, till they were *over the border* of evil.

And again, of Gudrun:

> *Cross the threshold*, and you found her completely, completely cynical about the social world and its advantages. Once inside the house of her soul, and there was a pungent atmosphere of corrosion, an inflamed darkness of sensation, and a vivid, subtle, critical consciousness, that saw the world distorted, horrific.

In both stories the thoroughly Romantic notion that man's spiritual dignity and greatness consist in aspiring beyond the finite and known and possible into the darkness of the unknown continually qualifies the openly declared horror of the darkness, and the notion that to go beyond the permitted limits is sinful, or abominable.

> He has to live in the midst of the incomprehensible, which is also detestable.

He realised that these were great mysteries to be unsealed, sensual, mindless, dreadful mysteries, far beyond the phallic cult.

But here the resemblances end, and I turn to consider the differences.

Heart of Darkness makes out a case for unqualified commitment, even to evil, and it is primarily about Kurtz the extremist rather than Marlow. ('. . . it is better, in a paradoxical way, to do evil than to do nothing: at least we exist'. So Eliot wrote in his essay on Baudelaire, and the remark provides a convenient gloss on Conrad's tale.)* The rhetoric is essentially a rhetoric of emphasis. Conrad draws heavily throughout on an arsenal of absolutes, categoricals, unqualified negations, superlatives and radical disjunctions; and the effect is to sanction obliquely the completeness of engagement, passional and imaginative, which distinguishes Kurtz from the captain-narrator, and attests the ambiguous heroism of his sin:

> . . . he had made that *last* stride, he had stepped over the edge, while I had been permitted to draw back my hesitating foot.

There are hundreds of instances of this rhetoric of extravagance or commitment; almost every page provides examples.

> There was a sense of *extreme* disappointment, as though I had found out that I had been striving after something *altogether* without a substance.
> I made the strange discovery that I had *never* imagined him as doing, you know, but as discoursing.
> . . . the gift of expression, the bewildering, the illuminating, the *most* exalted and the *most* contemptible, the pulsating stream of light, or the deceitful flow from the heart of an *impenetrable* darkness.
> . . . silly, atrocious, sordid, savage, or simply mean, without *any* kind of sense.
> By the simple exercise of our will we can exert a power for food practically *unbounded*.

And so on. One has to search hard to find qualifications.

* After completing this chapter I came upon Murray Krieger's essay, entitled 'The Varieties of Extremity', in *The Tragic Vision*. He considers the notion of commitment to be as central to *Heart of Darkness* as I do, but in other ways his emphasis is very different. To my mind he accepts the tale too much at its own valuation: he would clearly not endorse my view that the case made out for extremism is up to a point spurious.

And so with Marlow's account of Kurtz's dying moments:

> I was within a hair's breadth of the last opportunity for
> pronouncement, and I found with humiliation that
> probably I would have nothing to say. This is the reason
> why I affirm that Kurtz was a remarkable man. He had
> something to say. He said it. Since I had peeped over the
> edge myself, I understand better the meaning of his stare,
> that could not see the flame of the candle, but was wide
> enough to embrace the whole universe, piercing enough to
> penetrate all the hearts that beat in the darkness.

We are invited to admire Kurtz here for precisely that quality which
has previously excited Marlow's horror: the *extremity* of his engagement
with evil. Earlier Marlow had asked:

> . . . how can you imagine what particular region of the first
> man's ages a man's untrammelled feet may take him into by
> the way of solitude—*utter* solitude without a policeman—
> by the way of silence—*utter* silence, where no warning
> voice of a kind neighbour can be heard whispering of
> public opinion?

And he remarks of the emaciated Kurtz:

> This shadow looked satiated and calm, as though for the
> moment it had had its fill of *all* the emotions.

Kurtz has gone to the very limits of degradation and corruption; and
indeed this notion is implicit in the original conception of a journey to
the heart of the continent that at the same time is a journey to the limits
of experience.

> It was the farthest point of navigation *and* the culminating
> point of my experience.

In short, the story turns on a kind of pun. Kurtz is a man who goes
to extremes ('He would have been a splendid leader of an extreme
party') and the extremity is an extremity of corruption and, at the same
time, of imaginative vision. To a large extent the pun depends for its
effect upon that Romantic inclination to feel respect for the unknown—
a religious awe—which I have already referred to. But there is more to
it than that.

> We stopped, and the silence driven away by the stamping
> of our feet flowed back again from the recesses of the land.
> The great wall of vegetation, an exuberant and entangled

> mass of trunks, branches, leaves, boughs, festoons, motion-
> less in the moonlight, was like a rioting invasion of sound-
> less life, a rolling wave of plants, piled up, crested, ready
> to topple over the creek, to sweep every little man of us
> out of his little existence.

The flowing back of the silence and the flow of vegetation—a rolling
wave of plants—are indistinguishable, and as a consequence we find it
impossible to decide whether the jungle represents more a threat to
imagination or to sense.

> On silvery sandbanks hippos and alligators sunned them-
> selves side by side. The broadening waters flowed through
> a mob of wooded islands; you lost your way on that river
> as you would in a desert, and butted all day long against
> shoals, trying to find the channel, till you thought yourself
> bewitched and cut off for ever from everything you had
> known once—somewhere—far away—in another existence
> perhaps. There were moments when one's past came
> back to one, as it will sometimes when you have not a
> moment to spare to yourself; but it came in the shape of
> an unrestful and noisy dream, remembered with wonder
> amongst the overwhelming realities of this strange world
> of plants, and water, and silence.

There is an overpowering impression of fecundity and physicality, and
at the same time a disturbing hint of the invisible and occult (one
notices the image of the dream cropping up, as in Lawrence's essay on
Typee; and it is not only at this point in the tale) and the effect is to
implicate the seen with the unseen in a manner that bears very directly
on the central paradox about Kurtz, the man who is at once remarkable
and yet fit only to be thrust at the end into a muddy hole. Visible corruption is associated so closely with a mysterious, invisible life that we are
quietly persuaded to accept the notion that the physical and sensual
corruption of Kurtz (the wilderness 'had taken him, loved him, embraced
him, got into his veins, consumed his flesh') is congruent with immense
vitality in the imagination—that is, in the *unseen* Kurtz. Within a few
lines of each other these two passages occur:

> Beyond the fence the forest stood up spectrally in the
> moonlight, and through the dim stir, through the faint
> sounds of the lamentable courtyard, the silence of the land
> went home to one's very heart—its mystery, its greatness,
> the amazing reality of its concealed life.

And:

> I had my shoulders against the wreck of my steamer, hauled up on the slope like a carcass of some big river animal. The smell of mud, of primeval mud, by Jove! was in my nostrils, the high stillness of primeval forest was before my eyes; there were shiny patches on the black creek.

Physical and visible corruption everywhere, and yet an irresistible sense of concealed life. So when we arrive at the big moment when Kurtz has his dying vision, we are prepared to accept the possibility of a significant life going on in the imagination even after the man who acts has been brutalized and degraded to the very furthest extreme. The notion of seeing into the invisible is of course crucial in the story ('One gets sometimes such a flash of insight. The sesentials of this affair lay deep under the surface'); and so it is at this climatic moment—

> He cried in a whisper at some image, at some vision . . .

It is not conscience or enlightened intelligence that is primarily involved here; this is an act of impassioned and imaginative *perception*—with moral overtones. Kurtz's imaginative capacity, his ability to see into the darkness, has always been a large part of his strength, and now he witnesses for the last time to the depth of his depravity and the vitality of his imagination.

And yet, we feel, there is a trick in all this; something is being conveniently forgotten. A point made by Stephen Reid in an article on *The 'Unspeakable Rites' in* HEART OF DARKNESS is relevant here.

> It is all very well to speak, as Lionel Trilling does, of our attraction to the man who 'goes down into that hell which is the historical beginning of the human soul', but we become something more than uncomfortable when the possibility of *our* doing so presents itself. Conrad left unstated the specific (and therefore possible) acts of bestiality that Kurtz sinks to. It is easier, then, for Marlow to announce his admiration of Kurtz. It is not only that Marlow does not know specifically what the rites are—he will not learn. The point is simply that if one is going to admire the bestial in man, it is safer not to know too much about it. If the bestial is specific, it is possible; if it remains abstract ('abominable terrors', 'abominable satisfactions'), it is really only an idea.[4]

And the point surely is well taken. *If we stop to reflect,* we can only admire Kurtz's commitment and accept the paradox of his 'moral victory'* by dissociating the imaginative man from the man of action, the one who indulged in unspeakable rites. The former impresses us with the intensity of his vision; the latter is worse than a savage.

We make some such distinction, certainly, but we are not allowed to become too aware that we are making it; for if we did the character of Kurtz would begin to fall apart, and the quality James called 'intensity' would evaporate. But the intensity is undeniable for the most part, and it is the rhetoric that is largely responsible, persistently implicating or equating the visible and invisible, the imaginative and the sensual, and holding Kurtz together as a character even while the 'story', by implication, is busy disintegrating him. And the manoeuvre which Stephen Reid points to contributes to the same effect, outwitting the objections which commonsense would be sure to make if it were allowed to be heard. Yet there is something wrong with an artefact that sustains itself, in the last analysis, by trickery. And in fact the trick doesn't entirely work. Though Conrad depends for the resolution of his story on our tacitly dissociating the imaginative and the sensual, beyond a certain point the subject he is concerned with prevents our doing so. For it is a comprehensive subject, the human soul in the vast context of history and pre-history—no less. The river Marlow travels up is the dark river of time; and again and again the language hints at the possibility of a de-volution of the psyche to the point where intelligence, imagination and will lose themselves in undifferentiated sensuality. When we come to the climax of the story then, we have every right to expect that it will deal with a human being as a full sensibility, even if a full sensibility in decay. But it doesn't; and the puzzlement and vague sense of dissatisfaction which critics have shown in their comments on Kurtz's death are a measure perhaps of this failure to live up to legitimate expectations.

* I cannot agree with those who regard Marlow's equivocal admiration of Kurtz as a simple irony on Conrad's part:—for example,

> It seems perverse and sentimental to attribute to anyone
> except Marlow the notion that Kurtz represents a character
> to be admired, and his end some sort of 'moral victory': a
> Marlow, moreover, recording the disorder and fascination
> remembered from a state of nervous collapse.

(Douglas Brown, 'From *Heart of Darkness* to *Nostromo:* An Approach to Conrad', *The Modern Age*, ed. Boris Ford, Pelican, 1961, p. 137, note). This is to fail to take into account the extent to which Marlow's admiration is endorsed by what I have called a rhetoric of emphasis.

By contrast, the paradox about corruption in *Women in Love* doesn't depend on rhetorical trickery at all. Here the association of the savage and the visionary is altogether acceptable; for if Lawrence's savages belong to the primeval mud they are also the agents of a subtle culture ('pure culture in sensation, culture in the physical consciousness') and the creators of highly sophisticated art. We may compare this, from the first version of the essay on Melville:

> No man can look at the African grotesque carvings, for example, or the decoration patterns of the Oceanic islanders, without seeing in them the *infinitely sophisticated* soul which produces distortion from its own distorted psyche, a psyche distorted through myriad generations of degeneration.
>
> *(Italics mine.)*

The savages in *Heart of Darkness* however are *mere* denizens of the mud and have, apparently, none but the most rudimentary culture. The notion that their un-complex degradation could, however deviously, be a source of visionary power analogous to that of the Romantic seer would doubtless have seemed to Lawrence a sentimentality.

My main concern in this book has been with Lawrence's debt to English Romanticism in its early phase, though I have been led to refer to later phases from time to time—and particularly to later developments in the nineteenth-century cult of corruption. But further comment on these later developments seems called for at this point (though the discussion will be brief), since my present subject is Lawrence's primitivism and since the history of the key words I have been interested in is patently affected by the crossing of decadent with primitivist and apocalyptic pre-occupations in writers of the last decade of the old century and the early decades of the new.

My comments here can be even briefer than they would otherwise have been because I am able to draw upon a recent article that concerns itself with this topic directly: K. K. Ruthven's *The Savage God: Conrad and Lawrence*.[5] Mr Ruthven writes:

> The Savage God Yeats identified [*Autobiographies*, London 1955 pp. 348 ff.] is in many ways the epitome of a particularly intense form of primitivism that developed towards the end of the nineteenth century, merged with current anarchism, and culminated in a desire to destroy European civilization. . . . Savage primitivism (for so it might be called) is a destructive hatred of civilization; the savage primitivist envisages destruction as the only solution to

the problems of a hypercivilized Europe, and . . . generally
takes a compensatory interest in primitive peoples, particularly in primitive Africans. . . .

Page after page of [Lawrence's] *Letters* reiterates and ex-
pounds the same theme, often in imagery recalling the
book of *Revelation*. Equally apocalyptic in tone and origin
is Lawrence's concern with the new life made possible by
all this destruction . . .

All this helps explain the phoenix-like fate of the people
in Lawrence's novels, people who 'die' in some extreme
humiliation and then find themselves reborn, not in heaven
but here on earth, after undergoing various degradations in
the course of which their connection with the old world and
the old values is systematically eradicated. These degradations, it turns out, are degradations only in terms of the
old values; looking back from the vantage point of the
new life they see that the so-called degradations were
really stages in their emancipation, the ultimate degradation
being in fact synonymous with the final act of liberation.

I have emphasized throughout this book that in Lawrence's best work
the negative potentialities in dissolution are apt to be held in tension
with the positive, and at first glance it would appear that this is what Mr
Ruthven too is saying; for he speaks of a great positive swing counter-
balancing pessimism. Up to a point this emphasis is welcome; for all
that, it seems to me to be seriously distorted.* For degradation is not, as
this reading would suggest, a process that Birkin and Ursula altogether
emerge from, renewed. Something like this is intimated at one level,
certainly; but what is more pervasively suggested is that the two processes
—renewal and dissolution, regeneration and the descent into corruption
—can never in fact be dissociated; or more accurately, that there is after
all only the one process, the ambivalent process of reduction. Accord-
ingly, we find that every intimation that Birkin and Ursula are liberated,
or 're-born', is undercut or obscurely qualified.

Whether he is stressing the process of corruption or (inordinately)
the rhythm of re-birth, Mr Ruthven's eye runs far too easily past the

* George Ford provides a comparable discussion of the apocalyptic
theme in his chapter 'Dies Irae': *Women in Love*; but he supposes the
concepts of degeneration and corruption to have a largely negative
value, as I noted above (page x). Indeed Ruthven's reading and his err
in directly contrary ways: one underestimates the redemptive value of
degeneration while the other, in emphasizing this value, underplays the
reality and the ugliness of degeneration, the abiding threat to life.

text to the ideological-historical context. ('*Fin de siécle* pessimism is qualified by *nouveau siécle* optimism', and so on). Certainly, in commenting on the major novels we ought to note the decadent and apocalyptic preoccupations of late-Romantic culture, and the connections these have with the contemporary interest in the primitive; the writings of Frobenius, Tyler, Frazer, Freud, Spengler and so on have, for the critical purpose in view, a *prima facie* relevance.* But answers to questions about the *precise* kind of relevance are by no means so easily arrived at; notoriously, the danger of critical *a priorism* in investigations of this kind is acute. In Mr Ruthven's case, at any rate, the relatively casual attention he pays to Lawrence's texts, and his interpretation of *Women in Love* as an unequivocal tribute to primitive gods, seems to have a good deal to do with commitment to a prior thesis about the shaping pressures exerted by history and current ideologies. There is a welcome emphasis throughout the article on Lawrence's fascination with 'what civilization excludes', and upon his conviction 'that the act of exclusion has severed us from sources of great vitality'. What is wanting is the complementary emphasis: a due recognition that in the world of *Women in Love* vitality is threatened, above all, by the dissolution entailed in just this act of exclusion.

* There are some pertinent remarks on this topic in Northrop Frye's 'Yeats and the Language of Symbolism', *University of Toronto Quarterly*, XVII, 1947–8, 1–17.

V Mechanical and Paradisal: The Plumed Serpent *and* Lady Chatterley's Lover

The machine, inevitably, is *within* us: this perception informs *The Rainbow* and *Women in Love* throughout, and not simply in the sense that the individual, whether master or man, is conceived of as reduced in our society to a significance purely functional or instrumental. The machine is in us in the deeper sense that the great reductive principle is in us. The will, 'the greatest of all control-principles', is also the great 'machine-principle', Lawrence observes in the essay on Poe. But because in industrial societies this principle operates tyrannically it does not follow that the effect of Lawrence's art is to discount the principle altogether—to imply that it has no rightful part at all in our composition. In the discursive writings, it is true, he sometimes does go to these lengths. The essay *Democracy* is a notable instance.

> You can have life two ways. Either everything is created from the mind, downwards; or else everything proceeds from the creative quick, outwards into exfoliation and blossom . . . The actual living quick itself is alone the creative reality . . . The only thing man has to trust to in coming to himself is his desire and his impulse. But both desire and impulse tend to fall into mechanical automatism: to fall from spontaneous reality into dead or material reality.[1]

As an artist however, in his best work at any rate, he is far from suggesting that this is the whole truth, far from resting in this absolute disjunction. The fall into mechanism is charted in the fiction as early as *Sons and Lovers*, with a prophetic hint of the complexity of *Women in Love* but with some of the simplicity too of the essay I have just quoted.

> . . . As a rule, when he started love-making, the emotion was strong enough to carry with it everything—reason, soul, blood—in a great sweep, like the Trent carries bodily its back-swirls and intertwinings, noiselessly. Gradually the little criticisms, the little sensations, were lost, thought also went, everything borne along in one flood. He became, not a man with a mind, but a great instinct. . . .
>
> And Clara knew this held him to her, so she trusted altogether to the passion. It, however, failed her very often. They did not often reach again the heights of that once when the peewits had called. Gradually, some mechanical effort spoilt their loving, or, when they had splendid moments, they had them separately, and not so satisfactorily. So often he seemed merely to be running on alone; often they realized it had been a failure, not what they had wanted. He left her, knowing *that* evening had only made a little split between them. Their loving grew more mechanical, without the marvellous glamour. Gradually they began to introduce novelties, to get back some of the feeling of satisfaction. They would be very near, almost dangerously near to the river, so that the black water ran not far from his face, and it gave a little thrill; or they loved sometimes in a little hollow below the fence of the path where people were passing occasionally, on the edge of the town, and they heard footsteps coming, almost felt the vibration of the tread, and they heard what the passers-by said—strange little things that were never intended to be heard. And afterwards each of them was rather ashamed, and these things caused a distance between the two of them. He began to despise her a little, as if she had merited it!

The Trent performs a double function here: first it is an image of power and vitality, the flowing in of energy unsought and unwilled, 'in a great sweep', and then, in a shadowy way, it becomes an image of perversity and mechanism ('so that the black water ran not far from his face, and it gave a little thrill'). The black Trent indeed is recognizably, if only just recognizably, Birkin's dark river of dissolution. The iconographic technique looks forward to that episode in 'Water Party' where the rivers of dissolution and life are held together for our contemplation in a single focus. The sense in which the love-making has become mechanical is perhaps not quite as obvious as we might infer. There is effort and will now, and the indulging in minor perversities; but beyond this, and more drastically, the love-making is mechanical simply by virtue of being conscious. Mechanism is the only alternative to those moments when all thought goes, everything borne along in one flood; and the alternative is *wholly* unacceptable.

It need hardly be said that in *The Rainbow* and *Women in Love* the fullest justice is done to this conviction of the necessity for unknowingness; but the strength of these novels is due, as much as anything, to the fact that Lawrence is also prepared to give oblique acceptance to the reductive or mechanical principle. The bald alternatives proposed in *Democracy*—either spontaneity or mechanical automatism—don't after all exhaust the possibilities; there are kinds of human activity which partake of the mechanical and which yet have a value and a beauty.

> They seek the reduction of the flesh, the flesh reacting upon itself, to a crisis, an ecstasy, a phosphorescent transfiguration in ecstasy.[2]

This is sex as humanity in its post-lapsarian state largely knows it, and in *The Rainbow* and *Women in Love* there is little inclination simply to write it off. We hear a good deal of course about excessive consciousness, and that 'life of pure sensation' which is in fact only the devious operation of the fixed will—the will to knowledge:

> 'To know, that is your all, that is your life—you have only this, this knowledge,' he cried. 'There is only one tree, there is only one fruit, in your mouth.'
> Again she was some time silent.
> 'Is there?' she said at last, with the same untouched calm. And then in a tone of whimsical inquisitiveness: 'What fruit, Rupert?'
> 'The eternal apple,' he replied in exasperation, hating his own metaphors.

One is reminded of a passage in the essay on Hawthorne:

> When Adam went and took Eve *after* the apple, he didn't do any more than he had done many a time before, in act. But in consciousness he did something very different. So did Eve. Each of them kept an eye on what they were

doing, they watched what was happening to them. They wanted to KNOW. And that was the birth of sin. Not *doing* it, but KNOWING about it. Before the apple, they had shut their eyes and their minds had gone dark. Now, they peeped and pried and imagined. They watched themselves. And they felt uncomfortable after. They felt self-conscious. So they said, 'The *act* is sin. Let's hide. We've sinned.'

But if in *Women in Love* we are invited to deplore the fall into self-consciousness, imaged grotesquely in the figure of Hermione, it is also true that there is no espousing of Utopian primitivism in this novel, no crude flight from reason. In response to Hermione's weird lament over the children in the class-room, Birkin observes harshly that they are not 'burdened to death with consciousness' but rather 'Imprisoned within a limited, false set of concepts.' And this ambivalence informs the novel from beginning to end. Self-consciousness, it is implied, is at once corruptive and necessary—the mark of our doom-stricken state and by the same token our only way-through. And no paradox, we come to recognize, is more Laurentian. It is what the essay on Dana, for instance, is largely about (I quote from the original version).

> Dana's small book is a very great book: contains a great extreme of knowledge, knowledge of the great element.
> And after all, we have to know all before we can know that knowing is nothing.
> Imaginatively, we have to know all: even the elemental waters. And know and know on, until knowledge suddenly shrivels and we know that forever we don't know.
> Then there is a sort of peace, and we can start afresh, knowing we don't know.

In the Introduction to the Maurice Magnus *Memoirs* Lawrence observes:

> Humanity can only finally conquer by realizing. It is human destiny, since Man fell into consciousness and self-consciousness, that we can only go forward step by step through realization, full, bitter, conscious realization. . . . And we've got to know humanity's criminal tendency. . . . Knowledge, true knowledge, is like vaccination. It prevents the continuing of ghastly moral disease. And so it is with war. . . . We all fell. . . . We fell into hideous depravity of hating the human soul; a purulent small-pox of the spirit we had. . . . The small-pox sores are running yet in the spirit of mankind. . . . Cleanse it not with blind love: ah. . . . But with bitter and wincing realization.

In *Women in Love* the impulse to 'realize', or undergo the death-process, contends throughout with the desire to avoid realization. Or, to make the same point rather differently, a yearning to be born again—or to *avoid* the death-process—contends with a conviction that it is not possible to be born again, that 'the life that belongs to death' is the only life humanity will ever know; inescapably this is 'our kind of life'. Both beliefs are aired in the conversation between Ursula and Birkin beside the marsh.

> 'If we are the end, we are not the beginning,' he said.
> 'Yes, we are,' she said. 'The beginning comes out of the end.'
> 'After it, not out of it. After us, not out of us.'
> 'You are a devil, you know, really,' she said. 'You want to destroy our hope. You *want* us to be deathly.'
> 'No,' he said, 'I only want us to *know* what we are.'
> 'Ha!' she cried in anger. 'You only want us to know death.'
> 'You're quite right,' said the soft voice of Gerald, out of the dusk behind.

Birkin occupies here a position mid-way between Ursula's and Gerald's. He cannot share the simple faith and optimism of Ursula; on the other hand, though he wants to know death, it is not true that he *only* wants to know death, or that he wants to know it in Gerald's way (as that softly sinister intervention from the dusk aptly reminds us). Yet Birkin's position is not totally endorsed either. 'The new cycle of creation,' he claims, is 'not for us'. But this indefinite postponement of hope means in effect rejecting the paradisal myth as such, as Ursula angrily points out to him: 'You are a devil you know, really.' Seen in the context of Ursula's fine ardour, his attitude must seem at least potentially tainted. The whole chapter indeed is a most moving demonstration of the beauty-in-ugliness of the fallen state. To be caught up in the death process—that is, to be alive, to be conscious at all—is an agonized privilege; the process, after all, is a *flowering* mystery.* Without prejudice to its having the kinds of

---

* We need to distinguish here between the grudging admission of the beauty of the death-process which Lawrence is prepared to make in a non-fictional context and the far deeper commitment to this beauty that is dramatized in *Women in Love*.

> . . . Man cannot tame himself and then stay tame. The moment he tries to stay tame he begins to degenerate, and gets the second sort of wildness, the wildness of destruction, *which may be autumnal-beautiful for a while*, like yellow leaves. Yet yellow leaves can only fall and rot.[4]

significance I have already considered, Birkin's dark river of dissolution in the last analysis is the river of human consciousness. And we take this meaning even while acknowledging that there is a truth it does not account for—the truth, namely, that we are borne along on the silver, paradisal river too. This latter, indeed, is actually the river Birkin calls the 'river of *life*'—by which he means *eternal* life. But life in the sense of what we live by here and now, 'our real reality': the emblem of *that* is the river of dissolution.

It is a measure of the drop from the art of *Women in Love* to that of *Lady Chatterley's Lover* that throughout the later novel the mechanical principle should be so flatly opposed to the organic and paradisal. There is the machine and there is the sacred wood, and the 'symbolism' in terms of which the one is seen to threaten the other is of a crudeness one would have imagined the author of *Women in Love* quite incapable of.

> But Connie, walking behind, had watched the wheels jolt over the wood-ruff and the bugle, and squash the little yellow cups of the creeping-jenny.

The following comment has been made on this scene:

> . . . it is the machine which has revealed the nature of her husband to her, dominant yet impotent, asserting his will over the machine, turning it into a moral support, blind to the fact that he is utterly dependent upon it, morally as well as physically. ' "Thanks so much, Mellors," said Clifford, when they were at the house door. "I must get a different sort of motor—that's all." ' Connie looks at Clifford, and then at Mellors, and sees now the kind of opposition between them; she sees that the machine can indicate a dimension of soul as well as physical fact. In this, of course, we see plainly Lawrence's inheritance from a whole tradition of nineteenth-century social and political thinking. In 1829, for instance, we find Carlyle writing: 'Not the external and physical alone is now managed by machinery, but the internal and spiritual also . . . men are grown mechanical in head and in heart as well as in hand.' It is a contention which we can find as early as Blake and appearing in Cobbett, in Dickens and Matthew Arnold, in Ruskin and William Morris, and it is within that social tradition that Lawrence writes.[5]

It can be agreed that Lawrence is writing within this tradition; but one way of defining the weakness of the passage would be to point out that, alas, he is writing *only* within this tradition.

The reference to Carlyle here is worth taking up. If we read in full the essay from which the quotation is drawn we note that Carlyle bases his whole position on an analogical argument of a rather rigid kind. To become subservient to the machine is to exchange internal for external, to live entirely in the outward world, the reason being that the machine is an outward appliance.

> Men are grown mechanical in head and in heart, as well as in hand. They have lost faith in individual endeavour, and in natural force, of any kind. Not for internal perfection but for external combinations and arrangements, for institutions, constitutions,—for Mechanism of one sort or other, do they hope and struggle. Their whole efforts, attachments, opinions, turn on mechanism, and are of a mechanical character.[6]

Carlyle deploys his large abstractions and antitheses (physical-spiritual, internal-external, visible-invisible) with an undeniable if narrow power; but there is no forgetting that they *are* abstractions. 'Mechanism has now struck its roots down into man's most intimate, primary sources of conviction', he assures us; but his account of how this happens is incorrigibly schematic, for all the splendid vitality of the prose. Committed to inflexible categories as he is, he can convey to us little sense of the intimate inner life of which he speaks: that is, little sense of its reality as process or of its ambivalence and complexity.

By contrast, as I have already argued, it is just here that Lawrence's strength lies, and it is a strength that he owes in very significant measure to his inwardness with the native poetic tradition. Although it was from his Romantic predecessors that Lawrence took over the antithesis of mechanical and organic, it was precisely the great Romantics who make it possible for him ultimately to qualify and to subtle-ize that antithesis. In providing a whole new vocabulary for recording the chameleon quality of psychic process, the poets enabled him to plot far more intricate relationships between the vital and the mechanical than they themselves had ever envisaged. It is characteristic of them to discover an ambiguous value and vitality in the multiform processes of dissolution; and to these Lawrence now darkly assimilates the *mechanical* process. If the machine in *Women in Love* is a public and communal fact, sinister and lethal in the most obvious and simple sense, it is also identified with energies of dissolution or disintegration that are less easily repudiated, and indeed (as I have just suggested) identified obliquely with mentality itself. So we are allowed the luxury of simple rejections at one level but not at others. The 'disruptive force . . . given off from the presence of thousands of vigorous, underworld, half-automatized colliers' is not to be conceived of as sharply distinct from the disruptive, mechanical force that Birkin unleashes to destroy the deadly image of the moon;* there is a proper justice in his acknowledging that he too belongs ('in part') to the process of destructive creation.

The descent from all this to the art of *Lady Chatterley* is abrupt indeed.

> As sure as life, they would do her in, as they do in all naturally tender life. Tender! Somewhere she was tender, tender with a tenderness of the growing hyacinths, something that has gone out of the celluloid women of today. But he would protect her with his heart for a little while. For a little while, before the insentient iron world and the Mammon of mechanized greed did them both in, her as well as him.

On the one hand the violent and metallic and mechanical and on the other hand growth and tenderness and sex. And these steep contrasts are sustained for the greater part of the novel. Everything possible is done to dissociate true sensuality from force, to link it with fecundity, and by putting it in the context of nature's quiet and fluent rhythms, to give it a cosmic sanctioning. But we come at length to the climactic encounter on the night before Connie's departure for the Continent.

> It was not really love. It was not voluptuousness. It was sensuality sharp and searing as fire, burning the soul to tinder.

Clearly, this is very different from anything that has gone before. Wilson Knight justly observes:

> Earlier engagements have been given the natural sexual associations of softness, peace and fluidity, of floods, waves and undulatory motion . . . The new engagement has associations of earth, rock, the metallic, heavy ore, smelting, fire and savagery. The contrast is precise.[7]

But what is really remarkable and very un-Laurentian about this final encounter is the way sex is divorced, effectively, from its natural and cosmic context. For nothing has been done in the novel up to this point to suggest that 'this piercing, consuming, rather awful sensuality', violent and shameless, is sanctioned by nature as the earlier encounters had been. Of course there has been the engagement in the roaring silence

* See above, p. 19.

of the rain when 'short and sharp, he took her, short and sharp and finished, like an animal'. But it has certainly not been established, as it is in *Women in Love*, that reductive violence is a principle built in to the nature of things just as certainly as creativeness and fecundity. Indeed if this sensual violence puts us in mind of anything it is of the machine— within this universe of discourse the very principle of the devil.

> And necessary, forever necessary to burn out false shames and melt out the heaviest ore of the body into purity. With the fire of sheer sensuality.

We may compare:

> . . . greedy mechanism and mechanized greed, sparkling with lights and gushing hot metal and roaring with traffic, there lay the vast evil thing, ready to destroy whatever did not conform.

In *Women in Love* this secret affinity of the sexual and the mechanical is both exposed and endorsed; and the resources of Lawrence's art are exercised to the full to demonstrate that integrative tenderness and disintegrative violence can not only live together but imply each other. But in *Lady Chatterley* we have simply to accept this proposition on the novelist's say-so.*

---

* I find myself unconvinced by a large part of the argument of Mark Spilka's recent essay, 'Lawrence's Quarrel with Tenderness' (*Critical Quarterly*, Winter, 1967). Quoting a passage from *Lady Chatterley's Lover*— 'And it's touch we're afraid of. We're only half-conscious and half-alive. We've got to come alive and aware. Especially the English have got to get into touch with one another, a bit delicate and a bit tender. It's our crying need'—he comments:

> This connection of tenderness with wholeness and aliveness, awareness and communion, is new in Lawrence's fiction. Tenderness implies personal feelings, affections, soft sentiments from the conscious heart; and Lawrence usually speaks for dark impersonal passions from unconscious depths.

Spilka claims that in *Women in Love* affections are 'feared'. Even when Birkin grants love a place, he conceives of it as a 'yoke and leash'. The dominant effort in this novel is 'to preserve the self from absorbing intimacy', to get beyond emotional relationships to the 'real impersonal me'. Quoting the essay *We Need One Another*—'We are all individualists: we are all egoists: we all believe intensely in freedom, our own at all events. We all want to be absolute, and sufficient unto ourselves. And it is a great blow to our self-esteem that we simply *need* another human being'—Spilka remarks:

And if Mellors' sudden sensual violence is not prepared for or con-
textually endorsed, neither is his occasional spleen, or the recurrent
vindictiveness of the author himself toward Clifford. And here the
contrast with *Women in Love* is at its sharpest. For it is surely a defective
reading of the earlier novel that leads to the conclusion that Birkin,
set up as a norm of spiritual health and sanity, gives himself away not
only by his acknowledged sexual corruption but by his sick hatred of
humanity. W. W. Robson writes:

> . . . it is hard not to see in Birkin the Lawrence of 1916,
> amid the penury and misery of his life in Cornwall, and
> in his mind always the horror of the war and the nightmare
> of suspicion and persecution. How else can we explain
> Birkin's hatred of human life? 'Mankind is a dead tree,
> covered with fine brilliant galls of people', he says, and
> there is much in the same strain. But this is a defect in a
> work of imagination. Birkin's hatred is not clearly accoun-
> ted for in particular terms. It remains in the book just a

> The extremes of *Women in Love* have been abandoned. The
> new goal is relationship, through which we have 'our very
> individuality'. Lawrence has recovered his father's
> masculine warmth and wildness, has rejected his mother's
> egoism and relaxed his own defensive individualism; he
> is ready now for contact, for sprays and vibrations from
> living fountains, for outflow and inflow, for true human
> relationship. And so he writes a novel called *Tenderness*.

But is there in fact in *Women in Love* such a taboo on tenderness? Is
Mellors actually more tender than Birkin? Or Connie than Ursula? One
thinks of the love-scene in the chapter 'Mino' ('He enfolded her, and
kissed her subtly, murmuring in a subtle voice of love, and irony, and
submission') or in 'Moony' ('For a long time she nestled to him, and he
kissed her softly, her hair, her face, her ears, gently, softly, like dew
falling') or 'Continental' ('In her transport she lifted her face suddenly to
him and he touched it with his lips. So cold, so fresh, so sea-clear her face
was, it was like kissing a flower that grows near the surf . . . In a trance he
lay enfolding Ursula round about. His face was against her fine, fragile
hair, he breathed its fragrance with the sea and the profound night. And
his soul was at peace . . .'). It is true that Mellors *talks* about tenderness, as
Birkin doesn't; but that is another matter. And to suppose that we have to
wait until *Lady Chatterley's Lover* for a full attack on isolate selfhood
implies a serious misreading of *Women in Love*, as I hope the foregoing
chapters have made clear. To be sure, there is in this novel a deep distrust
of intimacy; but equally cogent, at the very least, is the fear of disconnec-
tion, the urgent insistence on the need for contact.

donnée, an idiosyncracy, which is so strongly rendered
that it seriously limits Birkin's value as a representative
of the normal man.[8]

Birkin's spleen may or may not be out of proportion to the given facts,
but Robson appears to be denying that any facts *are* given, that to
account for the spleen we have to go right outside the novel itself. ('How
else can we explain . . . ?') In effect he is denying that the vision of a
sick society, the vision of pervasive corruption and disintegration, is
imaginatively rendered. But I suspect that behind his formulated objection lies an unformulated one: namely, that the sickness of a society,
even if that sickness is rendered imaginatively, is not an adequate cause
and explanation of hatred on such a scale as this, is not 'particular'
enough. Some special event in Birkin's life, some fully dramatized act of
human treachery perhaps, is needed to focus his rage and make it valid.
One thinks here of the readiness of certain commentators to stress the
pathological aspects of Lawrence's own outraged and horrified reaction
to World War I, as though that reaction were largely incomprehensible,
and not in its essentials sane. In a vigorous essay on *Lawrence and the
War* Neil Myers remarks:

> The force which eventually produced Auschwitz, Hiro-
> shima, and the present 'tension' seemed to break right
> over Lawrence, shattering the complex fabric of feeling,
> institutions, and nature which Burke had celebrated as the
> foundation of civilisation, and whose slow decay Lawrence
> had already studied in *The Rainbow*. It created not only the
> famous cries of the soul in the letters and in Chapter XII
> of *Kangaroo*; it transformed Lawrence from a symbolist
> experimenter in the traditional novel into the compulsive,
> chaotic, half-comic propogandist of the popular imagina-
> tion . . . If the war made of the body of his subsequent
> work a kind of vast, sometimes incoherent *Waste Land*, the
> important point is that the effect is fully commensurate with
> the cause. If one takes World War I and its aftermath
> seriously, one must take seriously the Lawrence who
> spilled his awesome energy in reaction to it. One must
> take seriously precisely what alienates so many readers—
> the restless, angry disorder, and the interest in the kinds
> of savage energies that would fill the sudden chasm that
> the war had opened. The War made Lawrence an anarchist
> in all but the most literal political sense . . . To Lawrence,
> the use of poison gas or the 'bullying' of innocent

civilians are essentially religious crimes which, like man's first fall, corrupt everything associated with them. A society which creates and exalts 'that huge obscene machine they called the war' immediately breaks its organic social contract, dissolves its most intimate bonds, and sends men back to their original experiencing selves. Amid such chaos, one can choose either shame or loneliness. *Any* conventional act means a 'completely base and obscene' surrender to 'the dream helplessness of the mass-psyche' . . .

This vision is the source of the moral and aesthetic freedom in the later Lawrence, which frequently irritates humanistic critics.[9]

The features of Lawrence's style and construction with which Neil Myers is immediately concerned (there is no need to consider here the extent to which the post-war work is *in fact* characterized by 'restless, angry disorder') scarcely begin to be evident in *Women in Love*. It is obvious however that the war gets into the texture of this novel in other ways: at the level of metaphor especially the language is permeated by catastrophe and violence. Concerning *The Rainbow* Lawrence himself remarked in a letter to Waldo Frank:

I knew I was writing a destructive work, otherwise I couldn't have called it *The Rainbow*—in reference to the Flood. And the book was written and named in Italy, by the Mediterranean, before there was any thought of war. And I knew, as I revised the book, that it was a kind of working up to the dark sensual or Dionysic or Aphrodisic ecstasy, which does actually burst the world, burst the world-consciousness in every individual. What I did through individuals, the world has done through the war.[10]

These remarks apply *a fortiori* of course to *Women in Love*; in other words, the linguistic context is one in which Birkin's spleen can easily be assimilated. We need not hesitate to agree that the war does ultimately explain his hatred of human life; but this implies no imaginative defect. As Lawrence observed in the *Foreword* he wrote in 1918 for the American edition:

. . . it is a novel which took its final shape in the midst of the period of war, though it does not concern the war itself.

He adds:

I should wish the time to remain unfixed, so that the

bitterness of the war may be taken for granted in the characters.

Now there is plenty of bitterness to be 'taken for granted' by the reader of *Lady Chatterley*, but the bitterness is too often free-floating, unvalidated. At one time Lawrence was going to give this novel the title *Tenderness*, and there is a good deal in the text as we have it to suggest why. On the other hand the narrative tone is often conspicuously un-tender and many readers have found the note of sneering and bully-ing and malice in the treatment of Clifford quite repulsive. Their response is a further pointer to that failure of Lawrence's to integrate the creative and the reductive of which I have already spoken. The failure was fatal, for the destructive impulses always provided so much of the dynamic of his art. The *essential* energies in this novel are unambiguously pure and paradisal and for the most part the reductive or mechanical is a principle of sheer chaos and rigidity set over against the fluent rhythms of life. Hence the art of the cartoon strip:

> Tin people! It's all a steady sort of bolshevism just killing
> off the human thing, and worshipping the mechanical
> thing.

And it's no use pretending that this is placed, dramatically. We are told here that Mellors' face is 'pulled to mocking irony', but the categories are scarcely cruder in fact than those we have had to make do with all along:

> The fault lay there, out there, in those evil electric lights
> and diabolical rattlings of engines.

It is no accident then that Mellors should seem occasionally something of a prig. If the destructive can be so easily distinguished from the creative and so firmly located out there in the world of machines and country houses, it is to be expected that the character whose task it is to affirm the gospel should seldom direct his critical attention inwards.

In *The Plumed Serpent* the rejection of the machine-principle is even more absolute than in *Lady Chatterley*; and here we find, logically enough, that sexual fulfilment has nothing at all to do with will, or frictional voluptuousness—the 'phosphorescent transfiguration'.

> She realised, almost with wonder, the death in her of the
> Aphrodite of the foam: the seething, frictional, ecstatic
> Aphrodite. By a swift dark instinct, Cipriano drew away
> from this in her. When, in their love, it came back on her,

the seething electric female ecstasy, which knows such spasms of delirium, he recoiled from her.

Laurence Lerner remarks of this whole passage:

> It gives one pause to realise that the author of *Lady Chatterley's Lover* rejected orgasm. It hardly needs saying that Lawrence is inconsistent on this, that *The Plumed Serpent* represents an aberration in his thought. Perhaps one might have guessed this from internal evidence—from such a sentence as
>
>> Her strange seething feminine will and desire subsided in her and swept away, leaving her soft and powerfully potent, like the hot springs of water that gushed up, so noiseless so soft, yet so powerful, with a sort of secret potency.
>
> I do not recall any other occasion when Lawrence coupled together 'will and desire'—usually opposites in his vocabulary, the former forced and mental, the latter coming from 'the candle-flame, forever upright and yet flowing'. And it is hard to imagine any adjective less appropriate to the quenching of sexual desire than 'potent'.[11]

I have said something already about the widespread assumption that for Lawrence mentality and will are necessarily inimical to desire; but so much damage is done by the assumption that I make no apology for taking up the subject once more.

For despite what Mr Lerner says, 'will and desire' are coupled together by Lawrence, either explicitly or implicitly, again and again. There is for instance the passage in *The Lemon Gardens* that I have already referred to, where Lawrence reflects on 'the soul of the Italian since the Renaissance', on the supremacy of the senses and 'the will to ecstasy in destruction':

> The will lies above the loins, as it were at the base of the spinal column, there is the living will, the living mind of the tiger, there in the slender loins. . . .
> The will of the soldier is the will of the great cats, the will to ecstasy in destruction, in absorbing life into his own life, always his own life supreme, till the ecstasy burst into the white, eternal flame, the Infinite, the Flame of the Infinite.

If we lay this next to, say, a representative passage from 'The Industrial

Magnate', in *Women in Love* ('The terms were given: first the resistant Matter of the underground; then the instruments of its subjugation, instruments human and metallic; and finally his own pure will, his own mind') it becomes clear that Lawrence uses the concept of will in two distinguishable though related senses. There is the will to ecstasy, to maximum sensation, and there is the will to be master of life (or alternatively, the 'will-to-persist',[12] the will to inertia). Lawrence's attitude to the latter is quite simply dismissive; but his attitude to the former, as already suggested, is deeply ambivalent.

In the fifth section of *The Crown* he sets down as clearly as we could wish the grounds for his belief that the will to ecstasy is life-destructive.

> This reduction within the self is sensationalism. And sensationalism, of course, is progressive. You can't have your cake and eat it. To get a sensation, you eat your cake. That is, to get a sensation, you reduce down some part of your complex psyche, physical and psychic. You get a flash, as when you strike a match. But a match once struck can never be struck again. It is finished—sensationalism is an exhaustive process.
>
> The resolving down is progressive. It can apparently go on *ad infinitum*. But in infinity it means what we call utter death, utter nothingness, opposites released from opposition, and from conjunction, till there is nothing left at all, only nullity itself.

This is just the lesson Birkin preaches to Ursula beside the marsh: 'It is a progressive process—and it ends in universal nothing—the end of the world, if you like.' But I have, I hope, given good reasons for concluding that the process is a living process also. In other words, Lawrence's attitude to the conscious or willed pursuit of sensation, both in the novel and elsewhere, is neither simple nor predictable. After all, if the 'flash' or combustion, in that passage from *The Crown*, is exhaustive, the corresponding 'flame', in the passage from *The Lemon Gardens*, is 'splendid', 'eternal'—'till the ecstasy burst into the white, eternal flame, the Infinite'.

And since 'mechanical' tends in Lawrence's vocabulary to be a synonym for 'willed', it follows that his attitude to the machine, characteristically, is not simple either. One might suppose, from reading *The Lemon Gardens* alone, that for Lawrence the machine-principle is inevitably ranged *against* sensationalism, or the frictional ecstasy. For the machine is equated in this essay with spirituality, idealism, 'the Not-

Me'. There are two 'ways', the way of the machine and the way of the tiger, both valid, both necessary: 'The tiger is not wrong, the machine is not wrong'—the true horror lies in confusing them. But in fact, as I have indicated earlier, Lawrence is just as likely to *identify* the machine and sensationalism as he is to oppose them.

> In Poe, sensationalism is a process of explosive dis-
> integration, phosphorescent, electric, refracted . . . He
> is a unit of will rather than a unit of being . . . But the will
> is the greatest of all control-principles, the greatest
> machine-principle.

Returning then to Mr Lerner's comment on *The Plumed Serpent*, we remark a serious measure of inaccuracy in the suggestion that the passage in question represents an aberration in Lawrence's thought. The imagery is very Laurentian, to begin with (compare '. . . the beak-like friction of Aphrodite of the foam, the friction which flares out in circles of phosphorescent ecstasy', from the novel, and 'Aphrodite, the queen of the senses, she, born of the sea-foam, . . . the luminousness of the gleaming senses', from *The Lemon Gardens*), and the decisive rejection of the 'white ecstasy' is very Laurentian too. Moreover, it is surely imprecise (in reference to the way Kate is educated by Cipriano) to speak, flatly, of 'the quenching of sexual desire' and the inappropriate-ness of the word 'potent'. There is no obvious suggestion in the text that sexuality is transcended, though the fierce, frictional satisfaction certainly is: 'What happened was dark and untellable'. We are reminded in fact of *Lady Chatterley*.

> And this time his being within her was all soft and
> iridescent, purely soft and iridescent, such as no con-
> sciousness could seize. Her whole self quivered unconscious
> and alive, like plasm. She could not know what it was.
> She could not remember what it had been. Only that it
> had been more lovely than anything ever could be. Only
> that. And afterwards she was utterly still, utterly unknow-
> ing, she was not aware for how long. And he was still
> with her, in an unfathomable silence along with her. And
> of this, they would never speak.

In *Women in Love* and *Lady Chatterley* Lawrence endeavours, with very different degrees of success, to have it both ways, to celebrate two modes of sexuality: one that excludes the frictional or mechanical, or moves towards such an exclusion, and one that consciously embraces the mechanical. In *The Plumed Serpent*, by contrast, only one kind of life-mediating sexuality is allowed for: the *non*-mechanical, or *non*-sensational. And this is appropriate enough in a novel that is so uncompromising and Utopian—or, to put it more harshly, so apt to lose touch with common sense. (One thinks, for instance, of the crude and ludicrous repudiation of the machine in Ramón's Fourth Hymn: '*I see dark things rushing across the country.* Yea, Lord! Even trains and *Camiones* and automobiles.') But if the Utopian sexuality of Cipriano and Kate is appropriate in its context and in itself recognizably Laurentian, it is also, in a very different sense from that which Mr Lerner has in mind, 'an aberration'. For in the larger part of Lawrence's fiction the envisaging of a paradisal fulfilment, and the rejection of sensationalism, are always apt to be balanced by an equally decisive, if less direct, *commitment* to sensationalism—that is, to disintegrative sex and the machine-principle. And this 'larger part' of the fiction includes his finest work.

Whether any human being could, in fact, achieve a life-style in which these disparate attitudes to sensationalism were resolved is another matter. It is unlikely, to put it mildly; and in *Women in Love*, at all events, the unlikeliness is taken very much into account. Such completeness of being, or so paradoxical a fulfilment, it is implied there, is impossible, though essential. In other words we have to do with antinomies rather than with a resolution or synthesis. And yet, *through* the antinomy the ideal resolution is being glimpsed continually, an abiding imaginative reality. One is reminded, curiously, of the art of George Chapman; and a comment by a recent editor of *Bussy D'Ambois* is especially apposite—

> Thus the passionate search for an image of 'complete man', coupled with a recurrent recognition of his psychological impossibility, yields a series of conflicts of an essentially and profoundly dramatic nature, whose implication is clearly tragic.[13]

Conclusion

It has been claimed that Lawrence clearly 'intended Birkin to be searching for, and perhaps even eventually reaching, conclusions about the
relations of men and women in marriage which *could* be held to be valid
for normal men'.[1] But *Women in Love* is not, surely, a document of that
kind, not a novel with a message, not 'instructing us to adopt one course
rather than another';[2] we can't even say that *perhaps* it reaches conclusions, which is what seems to be entailed in the proposition that perhaps
Birkin reaches them. It is a novel, rather, that dramatizes that process of
living disintegration to which all of us in varying degrees are committed,
and committed most ambiguously. There is not a novel in the language
more truly exploratory, no novel less limited to the saying of something
previously definite. Ronald Gray has recently observed that 'Gudrun's
feelings and thoughts are as persuasively set down as though they were
Lawrence's own'.[3] This is true, and it follows that if we distinguish between the damned and the elect in this novel we ought at any rate to
concede that they have a great deal in common. Lawrence (Ronald Gray
goes on) 'surrenders himself as he writes to the spontaneity of the
moment, and that means surrendering as much to the spirit of one pair
of lovers as to that of the other'. And indeed from time to time Lawrence
approximates and partially *assimilates* the spirit of the one pair to the
spirit of the other. As we have noted, the licentiousness to which Birkin
wins Ursula over has affiliations not only with the sensual self-destruction
to which Gerald and Gudrun are committed but to everything the
African statuette stands for.

> And she gave way, he might do as he would. His licentious-
> ness was repulsively attractive . . . What was degrading?
> Who cared? Degrading things were real, with a different
> reality . . . Why not be bestial, and go the whole round of
> experience?

148

If Lawrence endeavours in this novel 'to blast through . . . degradation to a new health', the conditions for that health are located ambiguously in all four lovers; in two of them however, 'knowledge in corruption' ends in itself. So it is hardly profitable to say of Birkin, *tout court*, that he is 'sick'.[4] He *is* sick; but if he were not there would be little possibility of renewed health.

And this means that we cannot finally apply to Birkin the criterion of health which Lawrence himself laid down in *Pornography and Obscenity*; for it is too rigid.

> The sex functions and the excrementory functions in the human body work so close together, yet they are, so to speak, utterly different in direction. Sex is a creative flow, the excrementory flow is towards dissolution, decreation, if we may use such a word. In the really healthy human being the distinction between the two is instant, our profoundest instincts are perhaps our instincts of opposition between the two flows.
>
> But in the degraded human being the deep instincts have gone dead, and then the two flows become identical. *This* is the secret of really vulgar and of pornographical people: the sex flow and the excrement flow is the same thing to them. It happens when the psyche deteriorates, and the profound controlling instincts collapse. Then sex is dirt and dirt is sex, and sexual excitement becomes a playing with dirt, and any sign of sex in a woman becomes a show of her dirt. This is the condition of the common, vulgar human being whose name is legion, and who lifts his voice and it is Vox populi, vox Dei. And this is the source of all pornography.

We are reminded inevitably of *Women in Love*, by the difference as well as the resemblance. As in the novel there are two flows, two rivers—one of them moving towards dissolution. And as in the novel, dissolution is a downward rhythm and a regression ('decreation', 'deteriorates', 'collapse'). But unlike the novel (and unlike that other passage concerning the excrement flow which I quoted earlier from *The Reality of Peace*)* this essay opposes dissolution categorically to creation. A resolute separation of the two flows is the condition of health.

In the article from which I have already quoted, Wilson Knight comments as follows on the excremental complex in *Women in Love:*

* See pp. 18–19.

In what Murry calls this 'ultra-phallic realm' (*Son of Woman*, ii. 118) sexual distinctions are transcended 'beyond womanhood' in a dark 'otherness' at once 'masculine and feminine' (xxiii. 353, 361; and see xiii. 164; xix. 282). The technique may be called 'ambisexual' in that either man or woman may be the active partner:

... In his essay *Pornography and Obscenity* (*Phoenix*, 1936; iii. 176) Lawrence distinguishes between the sexual and excretory functions in terms of creation and dissolution, opposing their confusion as a mark of degradation. The terms ('dirt', 'flow', 'degraded') correspond with those used in *Women in Love*, though the concern is different. In his more imaginative and fictional excursions he is trying to blast through this degradation to a new health. Death and darkness—though darkness is used by Lawrence for more general purposes too—are natural associations, since the locations in question are those of expelled poisons and the non-human. So the deathly is found to be the source of some higher order of being; contact with a basic materiality liberates the person.

There is a good deal more to this effect; and all of it, so it seems to me, is faithful to the spirit of the novel. Daleski objects that 'it is difficult to reconcile Wilson Knight's interpretation with the description, as we have it, of what transpires in the public parlour of the inn', and Kinhead-Weekes, without actually referring to Knight's article, clearly has it in mind when he remarks that

... what Ursula discovers and responds to is Birkin's *complete* otherness, his wholeness in himself, by touching the fulcrum of his movement as an independent being. It would be farcical to call this 'anal' because it is precisely there to insist that what Lawrence is talking about is non-sexual in the usual sense; 'sexual' only in Lawrence's sense of the meeting of utter opposites, the light and the darkness in and between both beings. The significance of the coming together of man and woman is that this is the one way to contact the beyond, and the particular nature of the 'sexual' act is consequently of very minor importance. . . . Thus the scene is peculiar both because it is 'mystic', only to be understood in Lawrence's religious sense of the marriage of opposites; and because it is 'physical', since Lawrence will acknowledge no dichotomy between the flesh and the spirit. The oddness springs

from his need to create an adequate physical expression
for a mystic relationship—an embodiment that will be
'finally, mystically-physically satisfying'.

I think there is no question that Wilson Knight's reading is the more
accurate. He does full justice to the truths to which Kinhead-Weekes
draws attention ('So the deathly is found to be the source of some higher
order of being'), yet does so without losing sight of the fact that the
impersonal integration is rooted in corruption ('Through touch of the
impersonal roots, the centres of corruption and death, death itself being
an 'inhuman otherness' . . ., the true integration is accomplished'). As
I remarked earlier, the imagery here is linked with recurrent images of
downward movement, dissolution and degradation in the novel as a
whole, and Wilson Knight's comments constitute an implied acknow-
ledgment of this fact. In spirit* at any rate the interest is focussed very
much in the way he suggests; Birkin rightly recognizes in himself
inclinations towards perversity and corruption. But this is only to say
again what I have already said quite frequently enough: that the
characters in *Women in Love* are all of them caught up in the reductive
process, and that this process is a deeply ambiguous one. Gerald and
Gudrun give evidence of this ambiguity more emphatically even than
Birkin, and more disturbingly. To say this is not to avail oneself of a
cliché about sinners in fiction being more alive than saints. It is a way of
affirming that these characters cannot but be closest to the heart of a
novel that is engaged as deeply as this one with paradoxes about degradation. In his monograph on *D. H. Lawrence as a Literary Critic* David
Gordon remarks:

> The critic's prophetic reading of Dostoievsky and Poe is
> more ambiguous [than his reading of Hawthorne, Melville,
> and Whitman]. *The Idiot* and 'Ligeia' are profound
> exposures of the bankruptcy of the egoistic love-ideal. But
> Lawrence wavers as to whether the artistic impulse that
> informs them is truly physical and sensual or merely
> nervous and intellectual, as to whether it is the needed
> reduction *of* the ego or merely reduction *within* the ego.

True; and yet an equivalent ambiguity or wavering, an ambivalence of

* Daleski's objections, in particular, are somewhat literal-minded,
surely; he claims in effect that if there is anything abnormal in the sexual
behaviour of the lovers in the public parlour, it is of so tentative a kind
as not to justify us in calling it sodomy, and that in any case sodomy would
not be practised in so public a place.

attitude towards the reductive processes, is precisely the *strength* of the fiction, very often. Certainly it does much to account for the power of *Women in Love*. Again and again we are required to confront the disturbing truth that a reduction *of* the ego is being effected by reduction *within* the ego. At every level, moreover, we are prevented from making easy distinctions between the two processes. So that the ending of the novel, with its moving tentativeness, is more subtly appropriate than is commonly recognized. For none of the characters has been more involved in the reductive process than Gerald; so how should Birkin's attitude at the end be anything but uncertain, and deeply divided? Gerald turns to ice; he becomes to the outward eye what inwardly he has been all along, a worshipper of the snow-white abstraction. And yet Birkin mourns for him inconsolably, as for the loss of something quite inexpressibly valuable. Nor is Gudrun an awful warning, merely. Certainly the goodness, the holiness, the desire for creation and productive happiness have by the end quite lapsed in her. But that only gives the measure of her tragedy; for throughout most of the story she has witnessed to the deep involvement of the dying with the living, and to the bitter beauty of decay.

Notes

Introduction

1. See 'Post-Leavis Lawrence Critics', Mark Spilka, *Modern Language Quarterly*, XXV, 212–17.
2. *Double Measure*, Holt, Rinehart and Winston, 1965, p. 168.
3. The article is by Robert L. Chamberlain, *PMLA*, September 1963.
4. 'Lawrence, Joyce and Powys', *Essays in Criticism*, October 1961.
5. See 'The Marble and the Statue: The Exploratory Imagination of D. H. Lawrence' in *Imagined Worlds*, Essays on some English Novels and Novelists in Honour of John Butt, ed. Maynard Mack and Ian Gregor, Methuen, 1968, pp. 371–418.
6. See in particular pp. 398, 403 and 407. Though it is his main thesis that 'the whole process of recreation through disintegration . . . is central to *Women in Love*' (p. 411), Kinhead-Weekes fails throughout to note that this applies equally to the process of *reduction*.
7. *Critical Quarterly*, vol. 10, nos. 1 and 2, pp. 14–38.
8. Herbert Lindenberger's 'Lawrence and the Romantic Tradition', in *A D. H. Lawrence Miscellany*, ed. Moore, Carbondale, 1959, is, regrettably, not helpful at all. There is a brief reference to the topic in Leavi's *Revaluation* (Chatto, 1936, pp. 165–6).

Part I *'Dissolve, and quite forget'*: *A Tradition of Metaphor*

I Self-destroying

1. In 'Hymns in a Man's Life', *Assorted Articles*, London, 1930, p. 155. The essay was first published in the London *Evening News*, October 1928. See 'Lawrence and the Nonconformist Hymns', V. de Sola Pinto, *A D. H. Lawrence Miscellany*, ed. Harry T. Moore, Carbondale, 1959.
2. *Phoenix*, Heinemann, repr. 1961, p. 679.

II Images of dissolution in Burke's *Enquiry*

3. J. T. Boulton points this out in the Introduction to his edition of the *Enquiry*, Routledge & Kegan Paul, 1958.

III Abstraction and decay

4. From Lawrence's review of *Bottom Dogs* by Edward Dahlberg, *Phoenix*, p. 270.
5. *Phoenix*, p. 561.
6. *Letters*, ed. Huxley, p. 238.
7. *Ibid.*, p. 313.
8. *Ibid.*, p. 326.

IV Living disintegration

9. The distortion that results from stressing the prose tradition to the exclusion of the poetic is well illustrated in Raymond Williams' chapter on Lawrence in *Culture and Society 1780–1950* (Chatto, 1958). Mr. Williams concerns himself very directly with Lawrence's handling of what he calls 'the continuing key words': 'mechanical, disintegrated, amorphous'. It must be said however that he has little perception of Lawrence's originality in this area. The passages he chooses for comment are all taken from essays; he leaves the novels virtually out of account, and is unaware of how misleading this procedure is. (This judgment is confirmed by the tenor of the commentary on *Women in Love* in his later book, *Modern Tragedy*, Chatto, 1966.

10. *Apropos of Lady Chatterley's Lover*; London, 1930, repr. in *Sex, Literature and Censorship*, ed. Harry T. Moore, London, 1955 and in *Phoenix II*, ed. Warren Roberts and Harry T. Moore, London, 1968.

11. From the uncollected essay 'Edgar Allen Poe', *The Symbolic Meaning*: The Uncollected Versions of *Studies in Classic American Literature*, ed. Armin Arnold, London, 1962, pp. 116–19.

12. *The Crown* first appeared in three numbers of *Signature* during October and November 1915; it was later included in *Reflections on the Death of a Porcupine and Other Essays*, Philadelphia, 1925, repr. 1963, Indiana. It is also reprinted in *Phoenix II*.

V Intensification-in-reduction

13. *The Excursion*, Book I, l. 205 pp.

14. What I have said in *Romantic Paradox* about the ambiguous status of the Wordsworthian 'form' does not seem to me to be affected by Professor H. W. Piper's demonstration in *The Active Universe* (London, 1962) that the French *philosophes* thought of 'forms' as 'organized bodies of sentient matter' and that Wordsworth knew their work inwardly. It still seems to me that, qua poet, Wordsworth conceived of forms as ambiguous images, at once substantial and insubstantial, spiritual and corporeal. That is, qua poet he is a good deal more conservative-minded than Professor Piper's argument suggests. If Wordsworth believed with his reason that there is no 'solidity' in nature but only energy (a belief at that time very much in the air), his poetry proves nevertheless that the distinction between solid substance and tenuous spirit was very real to him—

and remained real even when the poetry *also* had the affect of cancelling that distinction.

VI 'Dissolves, diffuses, dissipates'

15. 'Coleridge's "True and Original Realism" ', *Durham University Journal*, March 1961. I quoted this essay in *Romantic Paradox*, but there I accepted the argument without reservations.

VII Flux and irony

16. See H. M. Daleski, *The Forked Flame*, Faber, p. 158.

VIII The downward rhythm

17. *Women in Love*, p. 103.
18. *Ibid*, p. 117.
19. *Ibid*, p. 214.
20. *Ibid*, p. 286.
21. *Ibid*, p. 482.
22. *Ibid*, p. 508.
23. *Ibid*, p. 508.
24. *Ibid*, p. 48.
25. *Ibid*, p. 193.
26. *Ibid*, p. 285.
27. *Ibid*, p. 286.
28. *Ibid*, p. 323.
29. *Ibid*, p. 356.
30. *The Rainbow*, p. 237.

Part II *The Activity of Departure*

I Reductive Energy in *The Rainbow*

1. *Ibid*, p. 121 ff.
2. 'Morality and the Novel', *Phoenix*, p. 528.
3. *Ibid*, p. 97 ff.
4. Daleski has already taken Leavis up on this point, though in different terms (*Ibid*, p. 97 ff).
5. *Modern Fiction Studies*, vol. V, 1959–60, i, 29–38.
6. I quote from Sale's essay.
7. *The Rainbow*, p. 237.
8. E. T. (Jessie Chambers), *D. H. Lawrence, A Personal Record*, Cape, 1935, p. 127–8.
9. Daleski, *Ibid*, p. 112–13.
10. '*The Rainbow:* Fiddle-Bow and Sand', *Essays in Criticism*, October 1961.
11. *Ibid*, p. 108.
12. *The Life and Works of D. H. Lawrence*, Harry T. Moore, Allen & Unwin, 1951, p. 141.
13. The passage quoted occurs in the essay referred to above, *The Rainbow*: 'Fiddle-Bow and Sand'.

14. *The Rainbow;* p. 351: see above p. 69.

II *Women in Love:* The Rhetoric of Corruption
   1. See *The Symbolic Meaning,* p. 126.
   2. *Phoenix,* p. 135.
   3. *The Collected Letters,* ed. Moore, pp. 851–2.
   4. *The Art of D. H. Lawrence,* Keith Sagar, London, 1966, p. 83.
   5. *The Symbolic Meaning,* p. 127.
   6. See K. K. Ruthven's essay on *The Savage God: Conrad and Lawrence* in *Critical Quarterly,* vol. 10, pp. 39–54.
   7. *Ibid,* p. 176.

III *Women in Love:* Individuality and belonging
   1. *The Forked Flame,* p. 181.
   2. These phrases come from the essay '. . . Love was once a little boy', *Reflections on the Death of a Porcupine,* p. 180.
   3. *Ibid,* p. 132.
   4. *The Collected Letters,* ed. Moore, p. 360.
   5. *Reflections on the Death of a Porcupine,* p. 176. ff.
   6. See L. G. Salingar's essay on Coleridge in the Volume *From Blake to Byron,* vol. 5, Guide to English Literature, ed. Boris Ford, Penguin, 1957.
   7. M. H. Abrams, *The Mirror and the Lamp,* New York, 1953, p. 68.
   8. *Phoenix,* pp. 541–3.
   9. See *Romantic Image,* Frank Kermode, London, 1957, Ch. I.
   10. *Women in Love,* p. 287.
   11. *Phoenix,* p. 154.
   12. *Son of Woman,* London, 1931, repr. 1936, p. 118.
   13. *Ibid,* p. 180.
   14. *The Dark Sun,* London, 1956, p. 79.
   15. *The Tragic Vision,* Murray Krieger, Chicago and London, 1960, pp. 37–49.
   16. *Phoenix,* pp. 377–82.
   17. 'The Crown', *Reflections on the Death of a Porcupine,* p. 74.

IV Savage Visionaries
   1. *Phoenix,* p. 525.
   2. *Ibid,* p. 267.
   3. *Phoenix,* pp. 406–7.
   4. *Modern Fiction Studies,* vol. 9, pp. 347–56.
   5. *Critical Quarterly,* vol. 10, nos. 1 and 2, pp. 39–54.

V Mechanical and Paradisal: *The Plumed Serpent* and *Lady Chatterley's Lover*
   1. *Phoenix,* p. 712.
   2. 'The Lemon Gardens', *Twilight in Italy.* See above p. 76.
   3. *Studies in Classic American Literature,* Ch. VII, 'Nathaniel Hawthorne and *The Scarlet Letter*'.

4. 'The Novel and the Feelings', *Phoenix*, p. 758 (Italics mine).
5. From Ian Gregor's essay on *Lady Chatterley's Lover* in *The Moral and the Story*, London, 1962. The influence of Raymond Williams is transparent here: see above, p. 154.
6. 'Signs of the Times', *Critical and Miscellaneous Essays*, vol. II, London, 1899, p. 63.
7. 'Lawrence, Joyce and Powys', *Essays in Criticism*, 1961, p. 403.
8. 'Women in Love', in *The Modern Age*, Penguin, 1961.
9. *Criticism*, Winter 1962.
10. *The Collected Letters*, ed. Moore, p. 519.
11. *The Truthtellers: Jane Austen, George Eliot, D. H. Lawrence*, Chatto, 1967, p. 176.
12. This quotation is taken from the fifth section of *The Crown*.
13. *Bussy D'Ambois*, George Chapman, ed. Nicholas Brooke, Methuen, 1964, p. xxiv.

Conclusion
1. W. W. Robson, *ibid*, p. 300.
2. From Ronald Gray's Chapter on *Women in Love* in *The German Tradition in Literature 1871–1945*, Cambridge, 1965.
3. *Ibid*, p. 352.
4. W. W. Robson, *ibid*, p. 299.

Index